ON THE WATERS

ON THE WATERS

The Joys of Fly-Fishing

RAYMOND W. KUCHARSKI

iUniverse, Inc.
Bloomington

ON THE WATERS
The Joys of Fly-Fishing

iUniverse books may be ordered through booksellers or by contacting:

iUniverse
1663 Liberty Drive
Bloomington, IN 47403
www.iuniverse.com
1-800-Authors (1-800-288-4677)

Because of the dynamic nature of the Internet, any web addresses or links contained in this book may have changed since publication and may no longer be valid. The views expressed in this work are solely those of the author and do not necessarily reflect the views of the publisher, and the publisher hereby disclaims any responsibility for them.

ISBN: 978-1-4620-6987-3 (sc)
ISBN: 978-1-4620-6988-0 (ebk)

Printed in the United States of America

iUniverse rev. date: 12/01/2011

I would like to dedicate this book to my wife, Patricia, who encouraged and supported my time researching this material, writing my stories, and especially for her proofreading talents. Special thanks to my fishing companions, who accompanied me on my adventures.

Contents

Foreword

To read these short essays of fishing adventures by Ray Kucharski, you come to appreciate the joy he gets from each fishing day and each cast he makes. The stories are not only charming but also informative about ways of catching the wily fish. Each story describes the delight that an avid fisherman like Ray feels for the sport of fishing. One gains many insights and some important learning lessons for life that this sport gives to all those who do it.

He describes his first learning experience of fishing with his dad, Walter, his mentor, and how he became "hooked" in the story "First Trout." Ray becomes "bonded forever to a new sport." You understand the deep love and appreciation he has for his father who gave him his first experiences and how their relationship deepened because of it in "Grand Lake Stream." Or the story "Brown Leaves & Gray Skies," about one of his early fishing days where the experiences lead him to become a full-time fly fisherman because of all he encounters in that day.

He describes the challenges of fishing: in "Tailwater Terror" Ray's fishing buddy, Jack, gets stranded on an island as the waters from the Moore Reservoir discharge outlet are released and how to catch a particular fish in "Dew Drop Inn." These stories not only talk about great places to fish, entertain you with the telling, but also provide wonderful information on where to have a great fishing adventure.

The beautiful descriptive detail of his surroundings and the joy, love, and gratitude he derives from being in the unspoiled natural world comes through in so many of his stories. "Coffee" or "Black Water" are examples.

Being an artist I particularly enjoy the descriptive vivid colors Ray uses in "French Impressionists" or "The Assassin."

The art of fly tying and the choice of colors or feathers he uses bring another aspect of the intricacies and the many layers involved in fly-fishing. The artistry in learning and making beautiful lures with colored feathers that will attract the eye of a certain fish in the informative story "Spider-Man," gives the reader an insight to the creative pleasure Ray derives from this fine art.

Practice brings skill over time says Ray. One gradually develops the skill of fly-fishing as told in the story "A River Runs By It." Ray points out you never stop learning, which is another reason the sport keeps you coming back.

Love and gratitude for the beauty offered by the unspoiled natural world and the creatures you discover there in "Close Encounter," or "Stalking Loon" or "Fishing Feathers." They are a few of many stories that show the humbleness he feels for the natural world around us.

He delights you with the camaraderie he forms with his buddies, Angel, Bill and others, the humility when the fish gets away and the optimism and excitement each day brings as one heads out to a favorite stream. The stories about eating a sandwich by the stream are a joy to read; an eating experience greater than a five-star restaurant. The plain camaraderie and bonding of friends that fishing together brings with the laughing joking and telling of stories; the near equal joy in experiencing triumph and defeat.

There is also a wry sense of humor in stories like "Crystal Ball," "Filthy Little Devils," "Open Water" or "Warren Hatchery."

I myself have fished, but very seldom. As a child we had a game my mother rigged at my early birthdays which was called

"Go Fishing." The birthday guests would get a rod and were told to cast the rod over a large screen and see what happened. My mother was behind the screen where she would attach a small gift and then give the line a tug. "Pull it in pull it in!" we all shrieked to the participant. Feeling that tug on the line was pretty exciting. Later I fished for bluefish off the coast of Duxbury where we got one bite after another. Aside from a few more fishing trips that were about all I did. I guess I decided at an early age that fishing was for boys. I read these stories with a new respect for those who fly fish. They exemplify the many things learned, and experiences gained from Ray's many adventures. Even if you are not a fisherman you will not be bored. I never was.

Ray has been writing these stories for over ten years for the small Waterville community paper, The Waterville Wig Wag. He also has written for *American Angler* and *Flyfishing & Tying Journal* magazines. My husband David and I, editors of the small paper encouraged Ray to put these many stories together as a group of essays. I am sure you will enjoy these tales of New Hampshire and New England fishing as our readers have.

Birdie Britton
Editor of the Wig Wag

Introduction

My father, Walter, had me on the water when I was knee-high to a grasshopper teaching me to terrorize sunnies and perch with a bobber and worms.

One day, we were fishing for pan-fish and were running out of bait. My father suggested I try a hook that had some feathers tied to it. The old-beat-up-fly had been on the bottom of our tackle box for a long time. I tied it on the end of my line and whipped the feather-covered hook out about ten feet. I watched several bluegills race each other to the "Brown Hackle" fly. Fishing was never the same. I was hooked, so to speak.

As I grew older, trout became the target fish. Walter bought an old wooden row-boat that was kept on the shores of Lake Quinsigamond, just outside of Worcester, Massachusetts. Every year the boat was put in the water early to give the plank bottom time to swell and become water tight. One year, Dad got hold of some special aluminum paint. It was so good, water could not penetrate, and the wood refused to swell. We spent a couple of days stripping off the silver-colored paint and repainting the boat. That boat was later replaced by a 12-foot aluminum "Feather Craft" car-top-boat and a 5-hp Johnson motor.

As a teenager, I became intrigued with fly-fishing. Paul Kukkonen, owner of Paul's Fishing Shop in Worcester, Massachusetts became my fly-fishing mentor. His store was half-way between my high school and house. After school I would stop in his store, and if he had time, he would sit with me and teach me how to tie flies. This was much more interesting than History or French.

I managed to continue fly-fishing through my adult life, but my fishing career was seriously affected by my working career. I worked as a structural-designer and later as a Design Supervisor at the Quincy Shipyard, south of Boston. I fished after work and weekends or whenever I had some time. I fished with co-workers that were interested in fly-fishing, and had many great experiences. In 1985 I transferred to Electric Boat, Groton, Connecticut to work on the, then latest, class of nuclear submarine, the Seawolf Class; and later on the Virginia Class Attack Submarines.

After retiring from my career as a Project Supervisor, at Electric Boat, Pat, my wife, and I moved to Waterville Valley, New Hampshire. My friend, Bill Gorwood, introduced me to fishing the local waters, and together we spent many hours fishing for trout and bass. Sometimes we caught a lot fish, and sometimes we got skunked. I fished with Bill for three seasons before cancer claimed him at an early age. He was a great companion, always laughing, never complaining.

Bill introduced me to Angel Carrillo, Allen Tailby and Jack Salivonchik, who accompanied me on many of my adventures.

Since I retired, I have more time to give back to the sport. I became a Fish & Game Certified Fly-fishing Instructor and Boy Scout merit badge counselor, and began teaching fly-fishing.

One day, I got a telephone call from David Britton, editor of the Waterville Valley, *WigWag*, asking if I would write an article for his paper. I agreed, and it was published in the next issue. The following week Dave called again. He said, "Your future articles should be around 400 words." "FUTURE ARTICLES?!" That was the beginning of my writing career. A year or so later the local newspaper, *The Plymouth Record Enterprise*, began publishing my *"Fins & Feathers,"* column.

This book is a compilation of those writings.

First Trout

Having terrorized panfish (bluegills, sunfish, yellow perch, crappy) and an occasional pickerel, I was ready to try to catch a trout. Trout were then, and still are, considered the Holy Grail of freshwater fish. Not rough scaled, easy to catch warmwater fish, but wily coldwater denizens of the deep.

I remember clearly, it was Easter morning; the family returned from church and had enjoyed breakfast, when my father asked if I wanted to go fishing for trout. I was ten years old, with six years of warmwater fishing under my belt. We grabbed our gear and headed to Lake Quinsigamond.

Now let me tell you a little bit about our gear. It consisted of a fly rod, silk line, some leader material, and a can of worms. Those were the days before spinning rods and reels were introduced. The only choices were fly rods or bait casting rods, and fly rods were better suited for trout fishing.

My father selected a spot to fish. It was an open space with a steep gravel bank behind us. We threaded a worm on a gold bait-holder hook—laid the rod on the ground—walked out a length of line and placed it on the ground. Picking up the rod, Dad cast the rig out with one continuous smooth forward motion.

The rod was then propped in a forked stick and the line allowed to settle to the bottom. A few loose coils of line were laid on the ground to allow any hungry trout to run with the bait. We then settled in to watch the line for any sign of a bite. Soon I was able to read the motion of the line, caused by the wind and waves. Suddenly the line jumped and half a coil of line moved toward the water.

My father told me to pick up the rod and place the line lightly between my left-hand fingers so I could feel the fish eating the night crawler. Dad told me—when the fish starts to run, let it run about three feet, then set the hook. I did as I was told. The rod bent double and a one and a half pound trout leaped out of the lake, sending out a huge spray of water. Pan fishing was instantly a thing of the past. My father and I were bonded forever to a new sport.

I caught my first trout.

Large Woody Debris

"See that overhanging branch dragging in the water?" my father (Walter) whispered. I nodded. "Drift your worm under it," I lowered the baited hook into the brook and allowed the current to carry the worm downstream. As soon as my bait penetrated a few inches into the pocket, the Bing-Bing-Bing of something eating my worm was telegraphed up the line. I set the hook and out came a beautiful brook trout, as black as a piece of coal from living in the shadow.

Later we came upon a tree that had fallen into the brook; again my father gave instructions that I followed with similar results. The heavily-forested brook we were fishing was located in central Massachusetts. The site has since been cleared to make way for Pleasant Valley Country Club, home to many nationally televised PGA Tour golf tournaments.

A half century later, Sandy Larsen, Chair of the Waterville Valley Conservation Commission, and I attended *The River and Watershed Conference*, sponsored by New Hampshire Department of Environmental Services. One of the sessions I attended was titled "The Role of Large Woody Debris in the Structure and Function of Stream Ecosystems of the White Mountains." Mark Prout, a Forest Fisheries Biologist for the White Mountain National Forest, discussed the effect of the return of mature riparian forest to the habitat for native brook trout. Streams were studied and charted; logs were cabled to the streambed, then studied and charted again. Slide after slide, using scientific data and statistical analysis showing least-square-fit curves, proved that Large Woody Debris (LWD) improved the trout fisheries. You can imagine what was running through my mind during this workshop.

The streams of New Hampshire's White Mountains are different from streams of central Massachusetts in that LWD is more difficult to find. New Hampshire's rivers were channelized and scoured out by the lumber industry after multi cuttings of the forest. The regrowth of the forest has not yet climaxed into producing LWD naturally. Finding a piece of wood in the river is like finding a treasure. It guarantees finding fish, but be prepared to lose a few flies. Every time I find a log in the brook, I remember my father's instructions.

After this conference I realized my father must have had a Ph.D. in LWD and its effect on trout habitat. Now I wonder when and where my father achieved his knowledge, but am thankful he included me in his fieldwork.

Fishing Car

A shiny-new 1956 Pontiac Star Chief sedan is not what one would think of as a fishing car. Usually it's an old beat-up, high-clearance truck or Bronco style vehicle, but this one was on its way to the Fish River chain of lakes, ponds and rivers located in T13R8, of the unincorporated section of northern Maine, just east of the Allagash drainage system. As a learner driver, I drove part way. At the Fish River Check Point, my father took the wheel to drive the rest of the way, on what the Delorme Gazetteer labels "Other Passable Roads."

When we finally arrived at the Fish River we launched the car-top boat and paddled upstream. We portaged the boat (think Charlie Allnut in the African Queen) to a secret pond that we were told held some trophy size brook trout.

We set up camp and were able to catch a few fish that evening. The next morning we caught a couple of brookies for breakfast. My father fried them and served them with left-over baked beans. Another five-star meal in the great outdoors. A couple of days fishing produced some large brookies but no trophy fish. Time to ride the current back to the car.

Back at the car we found a flat tire. No problem, those were the days when there was a full size tire in the trunk. Then disaster. No jack! Being that it was a new car, it was assumed everything was included. There we were, hours away from the nearest town, wondering how we were going to get out. Suddenly a Jeep came bouncing over the hill. The Jeep stopped and Walter explained the situation. The Jeep driver told us he also just bought a new Pontiac and happened to have the jack in the Jeep. What are the chances of that happening?

The tire was changed and we headed home. I got to drive most of the way. On returning, I washed the dust and dirt off the fishing car and returned the Pontiac to the black and white super car. I went on to get my driver's license and Walter got a car-jack from the red-faced dealer.

The Complete Fisherman

Now, I am not talking about Izaak Walton's *Complete Angler*, I am talking about today's complete fisherman. Every image of today's fly fishermen (and there are many now appearing in television advertisements) have one thing in common, a bulging vest and a funny-looking hat covered with flies. No, two!—Two things in common.

Ever wonder what's in those bulging vests? Let's take a tour of the content of my fly-fishing vest, with its 20 to 30 pockets. Starting on the outside of the vest, there are generally multiple retractors pinned to the front of the vest. From these zingers, hang a set of clippers, leader straightener and hook sharpener. They are lined up on the chest resembling campaign medals from some distant theater of operation. Clamped to a pocket flap is a pair of forceps, leading one to believe the wearer is a medical man. A bottle of flotant will be dangling somewhere.

The primary purpose of the vest is to carry flies. The flies are stored in boxes, known as Fly Boxes and hold hundreds of flies, some of which have not been used in decades. I still carry a pair of forty-year-old streamers. They are made using polar bear hair, and are so old they would most likely disintegrate with use. I carry them because the iridescent polar-bear-hair is no longer available. Usually the vest contains 3 to 5 such fly boxes. They are located in the large-billowed, lower-front pockets.

Extra leaders of various sizes, along with an assortment of tippet material are crammed into specially sized pockets. Extra reels or spools filled with sinking or sink-tip lines are stored in one of the larger inside pockets.

Next come all the peripheral stuff: a thermometer for recording the temperature of the water and air, tools to aid in tying knots and releasing fish, stuff to make the fly float and stuff to make the fly sink, a pocketknife, tape measure and insect repellant. A rain jacket is stuffed into the large-back pocket on cloudy days as well as gloves for cold days.

At the end of the year, as I cleaned out my vest, I found a half-eaten Power Bar. I find Power Bars good for a quick energy boost and as a temperature indicator, hard when it's cold and soft when it's warm.

For safety purposes, I include a compass as well as a whistle used for communicating with my fishing partner or as an emergency signal. I add a first-aid-kit to my kit. I may not carry it in my vest but it will be nearby. A pair of wire cutters for removing errant hooks accompanies the first-aid-kit.

What to put in the vest can be a weighty issue but this decision often makes the difference between success or failure, comfort or misery. Besides, the bulging vest gives the impression I know what I'm doing, and it looks good in pictures. All I need now is a funny-looking hat.

Rescue

It was a bright and sunny day. Another pleasant afternoon searching my home river for water deep enough to hold trout. Another year of very low water made fishing more like hunting. Plodding up the river, floundering over the rocks, I came upon a large deep pool tucked against a giant rock on the west bank. "This is it," I thought. The pool was about twenty by ten feet and three to four feet deep, a gold mine. My excitement quickly cooled as I studied the pool. The pool was isolated from the main flow by the low water conditions. Only a trickle of water flowed into the head of the pool. Dead water! I was about to move on in search of fish. As I continued up the river I took another look into the gin-clear water of the pool. My heart jumped when I saw a rainbow trout cruising the bottom.

I cast into the pool and BAM! he hit my terrestrial imitation. As I played him, my thoughts were, "good, now I can release him into the main river and free him from solitary confinement." I was a little premature because he got into some rocks and unattached himself. Double disappointment, I not only lost the fish but the rescue failed. As I watched the fish swim away, I studied the pool further and decided to return and free Jimmy (I like to get on a personal base with my prey). As I watched Jim dart from rock to rock trying to hide I noticed a second, much larger, trout tucked in by a rock. This larger fish was a brook trout. I will return, I promised myself.

A few days later I stealthy approached the pool again. My first cast came down a little hard. Jim and his buddy dove under rocks. "How could I be so sloppy to spook them on my first cast?" I thought, and shook my head in disgust and moved on. The following week I returned, this time from a different direction. My offering was accepted. "Rescue successful," I thought. I pictured Jim freely swimming away in the main current, forever grateful, when my leader broke. Oh, NO! I not only lost him again but this time with a fly stuck in his mouth. I felt so bad; I moved some rocks to enlarge the channel feeding the pool.

I returned a few days later to check out the situation. Jim had rubbed the fly out and was calmly cruising the pool. His buddy was nowhere to be seen. Lost to another fisherman, or warm water, or fallen easy prey to an otter or great blue heron. I sneaked around to the head of the pool and cast my fly in. A small brook trout, which I had not noticed before, darted out and hit the Black Zonker. Needless to say, his thrashing around spooked Jim and sent him scurrying under his favorite rock. I did manage to land the brookie and release him into the main river.

In October, just prior to the end of the regular trout season, I returned half-hoping Jim was able to escape with the higher water that came after some rainstorms and half-hoping he would be there cruising the bottom waiting to be rescued. It was dank and drizzly when I stumbled over the wet slippery rocks to a vantage point at the side of the pool. I put on my polarized glasses and watched the pool. I watched the pool for a long time, every rock clearly visible. Jim was nowhere to be seen. I guess I will never know what happened to Jimmy but I will be looking for him next spring.

The Stalking Loon

The reel screamed and the line played out, the rod tip pulled deep into the water—my heart racing—my jaw dropping in amazement. I have hooked onto the trout of a lifetime, or so I thought.

Let me back up a moment. Jack and I had been fishing for brook trout on Tim Pond, a small pond in Maine. We had been casting streamers on sinking lines, enjoying the sunshine and the surrounding natural beauty. Suddenly a loon popped up out of the water. We hadn't seen it coming, but knew loons could swim a long way underwater.

The loon popped up about 30 feet on the right side of the canoe. Jack and I shifted our casting to the left side and continued fishing. We shifted because we thought any trout in the area would go deep or swim away from the loon; we also didn't want to hook the bird.

After several minutes, I saw a large black and white shape pass under our canoe. The loon was now 40 feet off our port beam. Again we shifted our casting to the other side. The bird again swam under the canoe. We shifted sides again; I was surprised when my first cast on the left side produced a strike and a hooked brookie. I fought the trout until I was able to raise him high enough to get a glimpse of the fish. It appeared to be a nice size brook trout.

Suddenly, the fish panicked and dove for the bottom of the pond. The reel screamed, and all the fly line shot out through the guides. Obviously the fish was much bigger than I first thought. I was well into the backing when all of a sudden the line went slack. As I reeled in my line, I could see the Woodsman still attached to my leader. Jack was laughing loudly. I thought this very rude of Jack; after all I had just lost the fish of a lifetime.

As I fought my way out of bitter disappointment, Jack told me he witnessed the whole happening. As soon as I hooked the fish the loon dove down and swam under the boat and nailed my fish. With my fish in his beak, the loon swam off until the hook pulled free and the fish was his. The loon had been stalking us the whole time, waiting for breakfast.

Loons disregard all regulations. Limit catches and catch-and-release policies have no meaning to these birds. There are regulations protecting loons—must keep a certain distance from them, not approaching their nest, etc, etc. I want reciprocal rules. Loons should be prohibited from approaching within 100 yards of a fisherman.

There seems to be an urban legend that loons are rare, but most ponds I fish, no matter how small, have a visiting or resident population of loons. None of these loons are bashful and all exhibit the same outlaw behavior.

Beware the stalking Loon.

Remote Ponds

New Hampshire, and especially the White Mountain area, is sprinkled with remote ponds. These ponds can be anywhere from a few yards to several miles from any road. They all have that feeling of remoteness about them, no houses along the shore and little sign of human intrusion. Some contain wild brook trout, some are stocked by helicopter with brook trout fingerlings and some are too acidic to hold fish. It is always a mystery-ride hiking into these ponds, never knowing what the fishing will be like.

One day, Allen, Bill, Jack and I decided to hike into one of these remote ponds. It was located about two miles from the nearest road. Because it was summertime, we thought the water would be warm enough to wet wade, eliminating the extra effort of carrying waders and wading boots. We loaded our packs with fishing gear, extra clothes, lunch and other essentials we felt compelled to lug two miles uphill.

The pond was located in the saddle between two peaks. The water was low and the shore was clear of trees for forty to fifty feet, plenty of room for a backcast. The water was calm and crystal-clear. We could see bottom in twenty feet of water. We unpacked and assembled our gear. As I studied the pond for the first time, I spotted what looked like a sandy area on the opposite shore. I decided to hike to the opposite shore and fish my way back. This tactic allowed me to check the shoreline and depth of the pond. My buddies spread out and started fishing.

I got to the opposite shore; sure enough it was a small beach. The shoreline I had passed dropped-off steeply, the beach area gently slopped to deeper water. I decided to start with a sink tip line and a wet fly. I tied on a Picket Pin, tested the knot, and with great anticipation cast the fly out. After only a few casts, I hooked my first brook trout. The brookie had a lot of color—distinctive orange belly highlighted by its orange, black and white fins. In a short time I caught another trout and had a couple of other hits. I called my friends to come join me. They fished their way over and they began catching fish.

I decided to try a dry fly even though nothing was rising. I tied a Elk Hair Caddis to the end of my leader. The trout were not bashful that day, and they rose eagerly to the fly even though there was no visible hatch.

Not all hike-in trips produce fish, but they are all rewarding. Being there with friends is part of the reward. While hiking out, we talked and laughed and started planning our next trip to another remote pond.

Tailwater Terror

"Help . . . H-H-Heeelp," Jack hollered as he watched the white water inch higher and higher. Water was being released from the hydroelectric dam, threatening to cover the island he was standing on. Will the river sweep Jack away? Will the good guys rescue Jack? Sound like an old time movie serial?

Jack, Bill and I were fishing the Connecticut River below Moore Dam. We had launched our canoe a mile downstream at the boat ramp and paddled up to a rocky island. The rock pile was about fifty feet long and thirty feet wide and was located just below and slightly to the right, of the Moore Reservoir discharge outlet. White water ran on the left side of the island with a secondary flow on the right.

This was the first time we fished this section of river, and the island looked like a great place to beach the canoe and wade the river. The river was much too fast to fish from the canoe. We carefully approached the rocks from the right side and were able to successfully land the boat.

We lifted the canoe onto dry land and spread out around the island. Jack fished the secondary current and it was not long before he hooked a football size rainbow trout. We all caught these wide-bodied rainbows, with a few nice brown trout thrown in for good measure.

After a while the action slowed up. We discussed moving to the shore near the dam's water discharge. Jack said he preferred to stay on the island. Bill and I launched the canoe and paddled upstream the two hundred feet or so, to the shoreline just to the right of the fast water. Bill and I spread out and started fishing.

I was casting into the white water, letting the current carry the fly downstream and then stripping it back. Suddenly the fly stopped, hung up on a rock I thought. A moment later the rock shook his head and shot out of the water. The monster rainbow was landed, pictures were taken and the fish was released.

When I looked up, the river was roaring, the decibel level of the water was deafening. Not one of the three of us realized the flashing light on top of the dam control building indicated an upcoming release of water. We all expected a whistle or siren sound as a warning.

"Help . . . H-H-Heeelp," someone was shouting. It was Jack. Bill and I ran to the canoe and pushed it into the river. The current was roaring by the right side of the island. Somehow two inexperienced paddlers managed to get across the white water. Jack was waiting for us; he was now in waist deep water. Jack scrambled into the safety of the canoe. The three of us quickly paddled off the river.

In the future the three of us will pay more attention in dam controlled rivers, and avoid tailwater terror.

French Impressionists

The French impressionist's style of painting has always fascinated me. Their small subtle paint strokes and their use of unmixed primary colors to simulate reflected light, look like a jumble of color when viewed up close. As one steps back, forms begin to take shape until at a greater distance amazing details of the scene seem to appear. My favorite painter is Renoir, closely followed by Monet, Cézanne and Degas.

What has this got to do with fly-fishing you ask? When I tie flies, I like to incorporate the impressionistic philosophy. I use natural mottled colors. Red or gray squirrel tails and Hungarian partridge hackle are tied on the hook to form the outline of an insect. When viewed up close, the flies resemble a fuzz-ball. In the water and from a distance the shaggy form suggests the body, thorax, legs and tail of an insect. The mottled colors and shagginess along with the fly's motion suggests enough detail to fool a fish.

A secondary benefit to this approach is that I can tie a fly with a minimum number of different materials. Most of my creations use two or three types of material, excluding thread. An example is a long body nymph that imitates a damselfly or stone fly nymph using three materials; red squirrel tail, chenille body and Hungarian partridge hackle for the tail, thorax and legs.

There is a new art form of fly tying emerging, the super realistic fly, the Rembrandt style of painting if you will. These tyers will spend hours preparing a single leg of the insect being copied. An American tyer was traveling to Europe to show his flies in an international competition and the agricultural boarder inspector would not let his flies pass. Even though his imitations had hooks imbedded in them the inspector was not convinced they were copies. This new style of flies is not intended to be fished. The flies would, most likely, not fish well because they are stiff, off-balance, and have poor action in the water. These flies are intended for display only and sell for high prices.

Most flies tied today fall somewhere in between the minimalist, impressionistic style and the extreme realism of the show flies. New synthetic materials brings realism to the flies of today—Antron yarn replicating the air bubble of an emerger or the Krystal Flash imitating the flash of a baitfish.

As in painting techniques, there are many styles of fly tying. As in painting and fly tying the beauty is in the eye of the beholder. The difference between paintings and flies is that paintings have human critics, whereas the fly's final judgment is performed by a fish.

Filthy Little Devils

"If there's anything in the world I hate, it's leeches—filthy little devils!" Charlie Allnut said after he emerged from the Nile River and climbed aboard the deck of the African Queen and discovered he was covered with leeches. Most swimmers agree with Humphrey Bogart about the filthy little devils.

The medical world found uses for the little devils and fishermen are always trying to tie a better leech-imitating fly.

Trout Unlimited member, Dave Whitlock, lists five favorite leech flies: Wooly Bugger, Marabou Leech, Rabbit Hair Strip Fly, Whitlock's Chamois Leech and the Marabou Jig. Leeches are high on a trout's preferred diet and the high protein diet of leeches contributes to faster growth.

Leeches are annelids or segmented worms, and are closely related to the earthworms, probably why fish love them. Most leeches are sanguivorous, that is, they feed as blood sucking parasites on preferred hosts such as amphibians, reptiles, waterfowl, fish, and mammals (including humans). In the field, I have never seen a leech on anything but a human. Digestion is slow, enabling them to survive for several months between meals. Leeches breathe through their skin and do not require a high level of dissolved oxygen. They prefer alkaline water but survive in acid water.

Freshwater leeches prefer to live in still or slowly flowing waters, but specimens have been collected from fast flowing streams. In dry weather, some species burrow in the soil where they can survive for many months, even with a total lack of water. In these conditions the body is contracted into a round pea-size ball. A few drops of water and these leeches emerge, fully active.

In my experience bloodsuckers are black with a silvery-gray underside, but I have seen some chocolate-brown leeches and once saw a bright orange leech.

One warm sunny summer day, I was at my local neighborhood stream trying out a new marabou leech pattern. As the fly approached the shore I could see a rather large rainbow trout following the fly. When the fly got close to shore the trout slowly turned and swam away. On my next cast the scene was repeated. The trout was definitely interested but would not take the fly. On the next cast I slowed the retrieve. The rainbow swam to the fly for a closer look but backed away. When the marabou leech fly was about four feet from shore I let the fly settle to the bottom. The rainbow swam up to the motionless fly and gave it a nudge then slowly backed away. I twitched the fly and fish repeated its previous action. With my heart beating I gave the fly another twitch. The rainbow slowly swam up to the motionless fly resting on the bottom and sucked it in. This was the first time, and only time, I watched a fish take a fly resting motionlessly on the bottom.

I think I am beginning to like the filthy little devils.

The All-American Shad

Nancy Baker cordially greeted me as I stepped into the Waterville Valley library. I was starting my winter reading program and looking for a book to read. She informed me the library acquired a new book especially with me in mind and handed me John McPhee's latest *The Founding Fish*. McPhee explains the American shad's life cycle, commercial value, its contribution as a sport fish, and its history as related to our founding fathers. He informs us, "It was the spring shad run in the Schuylkill that saved George Washington's army from starvation at Valley Forge."

Shad, like salmon, are anadromous. They are schooling ocean fish, returning to fresh water streams to spawn. Shad, and salmon, do not feed when they return to spawn. No one really knows why they will hit a lure; why does a kid kick a can? McPhee describes various fishing techniques and takes a "catch-and-eat" approach to catching Alosa Sapidssima; after all it does mean, Most Savory.

I first heard about shad in the early sixties. Paul Kukkonen, owner of a tackle shop in Worcester, Massachusetts, told me about catching three to six pound fish, which got my immediate attention.

I invited my father to join me for our first shad fishing adventure. It was a cool mild May morning when we arrived at the Palmer River, in Dartmouth, Massachusetts. We parked near a bridge and proceeded to fish downstream. Not really knowing much about shad fishing, we took different approaches to catching some fish. I jumped from pool to pool not getting any bites. Around one in the afternoon, I found myself about two miles downstream on a pool loaded with fish. In a short time, I had my limit of six shad strung on a stringer. I was happy. The sun was high and the temperature had risen into the eighties. I began my trek back to the car lugging about thirty pounds of dead fish. By the time I got back to car, I was soaked in sweat and dog tired from carrying my load. My father caught his shad by staying closer to the bridge, waiting for the shad to come to him on their upstream journey.

Back in Worcester, we stopped to show Paul our catch. He took one look and told me two of my fish qualified for a Massachusetts trophy fish award. It was a pretty good start to my shad-fishing career.

Years later while living in Norwell, a friend asked me to take him shad fishing. After work, we loaded the canoe on the car and drove to the North River. We launched the canoe and paddled downstream to the junction of the North River and Indian Head River and dropped anchor. We each got a couple of nice shad. As we were about to quit, I hooked a roe shad. I knew it was big, but didn't realize how big it was until I had it in the canoe. Having no way of measuring the huge shad, I place her against my rod and marked its length before releasing it. Upon returning home, I measured the marking on my rod, 29¼ inches, WOW! The following week I read in the newspaper, somebody set the state record for American shad. The shad was caught in the North River, and weighted 9 pound 8 ounces, it was 29¼ inches long.

Angel

During my second fishing season (after retiring), Bill introduced me to Angel. Bill told me Angel had never fished before he retired, and took up fly-fishing because he thought it was neat. He probably watched the movie, *A River Runs Through It*, several times.

Angel asked me if we could go fly-fishing together. I reluctantly agreed, (I did not want to become a guide). We agreed on a time and date. I drove to Angel's house and found him waiting in his yard. We drove to the river, assembled our gear, and walked to the river. I set Angel up on a nice section of water and walked downstream about 100 yards.

I watched him fish the pockets, pools and riffles with a degree of proficiency that surprised me. I found out later, that Angel, a retired PhD research chemist, had thoroughly studied and practiced the art of fly-fishing. He became accomplished in casting a fly and even taught himself to tie flies in the few years he has been fly-fishing.

I fished the pockets, pools and riffles in my section of river. I fished the pockets, pools and riffles over and over again with little success. This river has always provided action, but today was one of those days the fish were not cooperating. I watched Angel patiently work the water with his fly. I felt that I had let him down, and did not put him on fish.

Finally I hooked a rainbow trout, followed by a small brook trout. Angel shouted congratulation. Just before we quit, Angel hooked a nice rainbow trout that jumped several times, before he brought it to net and released it. This was an exceptionally slow day, with only three trout landed. I felt responsible for the slow fishing.

Back at the car, as we disassembled and stowed our gear, Angel told me today was the best day of fishing he ever had. He got to watch me catch two trout, and caught one himself. At that moment, I formed an opinion of Angel that has remained to this date.

He reminded me of a lesson, I learned early in my fishing career. A lesson best put into words by, Sparse Grey Hackle, ("Nom De Plume" for Alfred W. Miller), "Soon after I embraced the sport of angling I became convinced that I should never be able to enjoy it if I had to rely on the cooperation of the fish."

The Trout Whisperer

"Your packages are here" Ann and Al said in unison. I had been checking the Waterville Valley, Post Office daily for the last several days. The long awaited packages containing float tubes had arrived. If you are not familiar with them, they are personal, inflatable watercraft in which you wear waders, sit in the water and propel yourself with flippers.

I had been debating with myself as to whether to get one for several years, but once I ordered it, I wanted it right away. Actually, Angel and I both decided to get float tubes. I did get to try a round tube three years ago and didn't like it. I sat low in the water and had difficulty controlling it. Since that first trial, I looked at newer designs, U style tubes and pontoon style tubes, where you sat higher and had more control. When I saw a new V shaped float tube, manufactured by Outcast, called Fish Cat 4, where you sat on a foam-filled seat completely out of the water, I knew it was the belly boat for me. These float tubes would allow us to explore new waters and provide many new adventures.

I quickly got the packages home, opened one, and called my friend, to tell him our kick-boats were here. The next day, I packed all the stuff into my Subaru Outback and headed to my favorite trout pond for the Fish Cat 4's shakedown cruise. It took about two minutes to fully inflate the double bladders. I strapped on the flippers, backed into the water, and sat in the seat. I was floating above the water with my feet hanging in the water, so far so good. A few flips of the flippers and I was off.

Most float tubers use long rods to compensate for being low in the water. I usually fish a 7½-foot rod, and to make the first trip a fair evaluation, I used a 9-foot rod. A few casts later, I was fast to a beautiful brook trout, a great start.

One of my early concerns was losing the intimate contact with nature that one has while wading the shore. Several experiences have dispelled that fear. I have had many loons swim up to me, and look longingly into my eyes, as if asking me to catch them a fish. On Spectacle Pond, a pair of loons kept swimming circles around me and swimming under my float tube. I finally realized they had a nest on a nearby island and kicked away. On a remote pond, I had a beaver escort me away from his lodge. He did it by swimming up behind me and diving with a tail slap. For those of you who are not familiar with this technique, the splash sounds as if someone threw a Volkswagen in the pond.

My most intimate experience was when a brook trout swam up to the tube and swam slow circles around me, as if I was his big brother. Fascinated, I watched as he continued to follow me around. On his third or fourth pass in front of me, I slowly placed my flipper under the fish and lifted him slowly out of the water. I watched him resting on my flipper for a couple of seconds then lowered him back into the water. I had become a trout whisperer.

Hard to Come By

It was the dog days of summer, and still water trout were hard to come by. My fishing buddy and I decided to act on a hot tip about a local pond that was supposed to be loaded with pickerel. The chain pickerel is a member of the pike family, often referred to as a freshwater barracuda. They are long, lean fish with a duck-like mouth full of recurved needlelike teeth.

We drove as close to the pond as possible, then walked down the path to the water. The shoreline was a sea of grass, about 50 yards of pickerelweed and another 50 yards of lily pads. "Perfect spot for pickerel," I said to my companion as he strung his 7-weight rod to accommodate the large flies we planned to use.

We launched our float tubes and made our way through the pickerelweed. The lily pads were a different story; it was like finning across a wet football field. Our legs were screaming by the time that we reached open water. We circumnavigated the entire shoreline catching only a few small chubs, golden shiners and yellow perch.

The next time I met the tipster, I mentioned our lack of success. He confided that he caught one pickerel, a 22-inch, 2-pound beauty, but it was seventeen years ago, and through the ice.

The next day we went to warmwater pond I selected from a topographic map. It looked great. The shoreline was a series of fallen trees with not one house on it. I remarked that it looked like a great largemouth bass pond. We spent a couple of hours working the shoreline, first with floating line around the fallen trees, then with sinking line in deeper water. Again we only caught a few minnows, which were not much bigger than the flies we were using.

Later, we drove to another pond. This pond was also reported to contain pickerel. We launched in a shallow cove and worked our way through the aquatic vegetation. I cast to an open spot in the lily pads and WHAM! a pickerel smashed my Chartreuse Zonker. We finned our way into the main body of the lake and explored the shoreline. After an hour of unsuccessful casting, I decided to return to the weedy cove where we stared. I changed my fly to a large marabou Mickey Finn and worked the open spots in the lily pads and managed to pick up a couple more pickerel. After two days of hard fishing, I decided that pickerel were also, hard to come by.

Adventures

ad-ven-ture n. **1.** An undertaking of a hazardous nature. **2.** An unusual experience or course of events marked by excitement and suspense.

A fishing adventure can be all of the above. To me, an adventure is finding and trying new waters. This year I had many adventures. This past spring my wife, Pat, had to attend a Town Clerk training session in Conway. She asked if I would drive over with her, and that I could fish while she attended class. I quickly agreed, as there was a fly-fishing-only pond nearby that I wanted to try. I dropped her off, and armed with a topo map, I set out to find the pond.

After driving around the pond, on dirt roads, for a half-an-hour, I stopped and asked for directions. The road into the pond turned out to be two rutted tire tracks through the woods. Glad I had a high-clearance vehicle. As I was setting up my equipment, I saw a few swirls in the pickerelweed along the shore. I launched my float tube and threw a fly into the grass and BINGO, a nice brookie. A short while later, I cast to the drop-off beyond the grass and had a tremendous strike. I put the fish on the reel and carefully played him as he towed my float tube around. Finally, I got a glimpse of the monster and was able to net him. The huge fish, turned out to be a 4¼-pound brook trout. Before I quit to pick up Pat, I caught two more brookies over 3-pounds and several smaller ones, a great day.

Another adventure this year was to the Androscoggin River below Berlin. Angel and I heard about it at the Fly Fishing Expo, this spring. This section of river was one of the most polluted rivers in the country. For this reason, the State of New Hampshire stopped stocking it. After the clean waters act of the 80's, the river water cleared. The state revised the regulations making this section of the river a single barbless hook, catch-and-release fishery. Because this part of the river has not been stocked for years, all of the fish were hatched in the river and were wild fish. Again armed with topo maps we drove around looking for places to fish.

We fished several spots, catching rainbow trout in the foot-long range, smallmouth bass up to 14 inches, and 14 to 17-inch white fish, a real rod bending day. We finished the day fishing below the Gorham Dam, parking at the recreation area behind the Public Works Department. After a long day on the water we hiked out, packed our gear and headed out to find some dinner before dark. Driving by the Public Works we looked ahead and saw the gate closed. We were locked in! We knocked on the door of a near-by house and got the number of the local Police Department. After a short wait a very polite police captain drove up, smiled and released us, telling us we were not the first to get locked in. This trip, marked by excitement and suspense, was an **ad-ven-ture.**

Dragonflies

Dragonflies and damselflies are aquatic insects that we are all familiar with. These were the "sewing needles" of my youth, scaring me because I were erroneously told that they might land on me and sew me up. It's fun to watch them hovering and darting above the water, then gently landing on a lily pad.

Dragonflies are the larger of the two; they have a stocky body and when at rest hold their wings perpendicular to their body. They come in various, iridescent colors. Damselflies are slender-bodied and fold their wings over their body when at rest. They are generally bright blue. Much has been written in fly-fishing lore, about the importance of dragonfly and damselfly nymphs, but rarely is the adult stage mentioned. I am sure there is a good reason, as it is very difficult to fish your fly two feet above the water.

My first experience with adult dragonflies and damselflies, as a food source for hungry fish, occurred many years ago. It was midsummer, too warm for trout. I was fishing a Cape Cod pond for bass and pickerel. As I waded the shore, I could see fish rocketing out of the water along a shoreline covered by pickerel grass. I waded over to that area to investigate the situation. These fish appeared to be jumping much too high to be bass. When I got close enough, I could see they were rainbow trout leaping high out of the water for adult dragonflies that were flying in and out of the pickerel grass.

Rainbow trout have a reputation as both jumpers and opportunistic feeders; this seemed to combine both characteristics. It was fascinating to watch them launch themselves straight up out of the water, or rocket themselves sideways, landing four or five feet away from where they came out of the water. The action was so fast, I could not see if the trout actually caught any dragonflies, but I have to assume they did or they would not have continued to chase them all afternoon.

I had not seen this situation repeated until last year and again this year, on our local water. This time it was brook trout. Now brook trout are aggressive feeders, but, unlike rainbows, not known as jumpers. These brookies performed much like the rainbows of years ago. They scored much lower on height and distance points, but excelled on style points. Applying lessons learned from many years ago, I knew I could not hold my fly above the water, so I selected a long narrow dry fly. A Cooper Bug in my box closely matched that description.

I can happily report this approach worked both years ago on the cape pond for the rainbows and for the brookies on my home-water. The fish would smash the fly thinking the dragonfly imitation would fly away, or the trout would leap straight up into the air, turn around in mid-air, and land directly on the fly with its mouth open. No namby-pamby sipping in of the fly. Trout feeding on adult dragonflies and damselflies provide for some action-packed, exciting dry fly fishing.

Lac Mabille, Labrador

The night was dark and the stars were bright. It was 1:30 am when the dark green van pulled in the driveway. Smiling, Charlie, owner of Charlie's Fly Tying Shop in Bristol, New Hampshire, stepped out of the car. A few days earlier Charlie decided on a repeat visit to Lac Mabille and was looking for a partner. Once he mentioned fishing in Labrador it didn't take me long to agree to join him on a trip I have dreamed of since I was a kid. We loaded my bag and gear into the van and headed north.

The route took us to Quebec City, then along the north shore of the St. Lawrence River. On the ferry crossing the Sagueney River, we watched whales rolling on the surface of the river. After 500 miles on Rt. 138, we arrived at Havre St Pierre, Quebec. The next day we boarded a DeHavilland Beaver and flew north 125 miles to the fishing camp.

The camp is located on a point of land above the outlet of Little Mabille Lake. The only occupants of the camp were Marcel (our guide), the cook and his dog Griffin, and Charlie and me. The camp consisted of several guest cottages, a dining and gathering building, a bath house, and accommodations for the staff, plus some work sheds. Wilderness boreal forests and frozen tundra surrounded the camp. The ground was heavily covered with mosses and lichens and walking on it was like stepping on a lumpy-plush carpet.

With the North Star high in the sky (54 degrees), and the Milky Way clearly visible, the nights were spectacular. On the clear nights, the Aurora Borealis danced in the sky. The northern lights appeared as soft green and pink colored spotlights moving in the sky.

After a hardy breakfast we suited up for the day. We traveled north by boat to begin fishing in Labrador's rivers. Lunch prepared by the guide usually consisted of soup and a couple of foot-long brook trout. In the afternoon we would fish our way back.

We fished the beautiful whitewater rivers for Reds (brook trout), Little and Big Mabille lakes and eskers (narrow breaks in a glacial ridge connecting two lakes) for Grays (lake trout) and northern pike. I had a wonderful time working a patch of lily pads for pike. The fish were not selective; every fly I tried caught fish.

I was able to hook some large Reds on my super light 6½ foot bamboo rod. We did manage to catch a few trophy fish and bring home some "Grip and Grin" pictures. I caught a 7-pound brook trout and Charlie caught a trophy-size pike.

We were scheduled to fly out on Sunday but the plane was fogged in, and we were forced into fishing an extra day. LIFE IS GOOD!

Fly-Fishing Through the Ages

No one knows for certain who, where or when the first fish was caught on a fly. There are records dating back to the third century. The philosopher Aelien tells us in his *De Natura Animalium* about Isaac from Macedonia, who reached into his earthen jar for a grub only to find he was out of bait. Inspired, he plucked a feather from a nearby chicken and wrapped it around the hook shank. This simple fly was the first soft hackle wet fly. Isaac cast it into the Astraeus and WHAM! He and the fish were hooked on fishing with a fly.

In 1496, just four years after Columbus sailed, Dame Juliana Berners, described methods of fly dressing and fly-fishing in a book titled *Trease of Fysshynge Wyth an Angle*. Angle is defined as causing an angle, as in between a fishing pole and the line. Some of those historic patterns outlined in her book are still used today.

Years later an Englishman took time off from civilizing the world and wrote a book. His name was also Izaak—Izaak Walton: and the book was titled, *The Compleat Angler or The Contemplative Man's Recreation*. Fishing has not been the same since. He wrote about "the dun-flie, the stone-flie, the red-flie, the moor-flie, the tawnie-flie," and also of the "caterpillar, or the Palmer-flie or worm". The palmer fly or Wooly Worm became the forerunner of today's Woolly Buggers.

In the latter part of the nineteenth century, American fly tyers and fly fishermen advanced the art. The father of the dry fly in America was Theodore Gordon. He cast his Quill Gordon dry fly, on the Neversink River, in his beloved Catskill's mountains. He dressed his flies in an impressionistic style imitating aquatic insects.

Theodore taught us to fish dry flies upstream and to keep a diary of fishing conditions and insect hatches. The theme of his work, captured in his journals was that, "The great charm of fly fishing is that we are always learning".

In the last half-century silk fly lines, measured by diameter, gave way to synthetic lines, measured by weight. Graphite replaced split bamboo and fiberglass rods. New fly tying materials and thousands of new fly patterns were developed.

Someone said that if we do not know history we are doomed to repeat it. But in fly-fishing and fly tying, knowledge of its history is not required to have fun. For like anglers of old—sitting down and tying some wool, fur and feathers on a hook—going to the water—casting it in—and seeing a fish raise to take your creation—remains the same thrilling experience that hooked Isaac from Macedonia.

A Fly for All Seasons

I stepped into the river below a deep pool and cast upstream to the head of the pool. The line fell gently on the water with a curve to the right, keeping the leader away from the fly. The fly floated high and dry for a few feet and a beautiful rainbow trout rose to suck in the fly. A short time later I threw a quartering upstream cast. The fly drifted just below the surface, another rainbow rose from the bottom and hit the fly. Later I moved to another pool. This time I cast across the pool and let the fly sink. A slow retrieve produced a nice brook trout. Next I cast downstream and at the end of the swing a small salmon that had followed the fly hit it like it was going to be his last meal. If you assume, as any fisherman naturally would, that I changed from a dry fly, to a nymph dead drifted, to a streamer fished across the current, to drifting a classic wet fly, you would be wrong. They all came quite willingly to one fly.

The fly is called the Cooper Bug. I first read about this fly in *"The Sportsman's Notebook and Tap's Tips,"* by H. G. Tapply. Tapply points out its resemblance to the Tuttle Devil Bug. In Maine they call the fly the Doodle Bug, and tie it in many horrible color combinations.

The Cooper Bug also has some of the characteristics of the equally famous Muddler Minnow. The Muddler Minnow and the popular Hornberg can also be fished wet or dry. For me the

Cooper Bug is a confidence fly. I fish it in both rivers and ponds. I know I can tie it on and catch fish if there are any around.

The original recipe calls for a peacock herl body and deer hair. The deer hair is tied in at the head of the hook, just behind the eye, and then tied down tightly at the bend of the hook forming a hump over the body. Clip the hair close around the head and push back the short ends so you can get the leader through the eye. I substitute a strip of foam for the body for better flotation. My color preference for the deer hair is natural tan-grey, because of its visibility. Body color does not seem to be critical. I use mostly size 12 flies, but carry a few smaller and larger ones. Put a few Cooper Bug's in your fly box and you will be well outfitted for seasons.

White Miller Hatch

Standing in waist deep water, I reached up and pinched the line and stripping guide until the warmth of my fingers melted the ice. This was repeated over and over until all the guides on my fly rod were free of ice. I had been repeating this procedure every ten to fifteen minutes for the last couple of hours.

The air temperature was in the twenties with the water a balmy thirty-six degrees. I cast quartering upstream and the orange cone-head fly landed with a splat and quickly sank out of sight. I watched the line slowly drift downstream. Concentrating on the sink tip line where it entered the water, I watched for any indication of a take. When the fly completed its drift, I slowly retrieved it. "Hitless," I thought, as I cast the fly out again. This time I looked upstream to my fishing buddy, Bill, and nodded "enough?" "Enough!" he nodded back. Vocalizing is not required between fishermen with like minds (especially when they are frozen). We both reeled in our lines and tried to get some feeling back into our legs as we waded ashore.

I had not been fishing for a couple of months and was having withdrawal symptoms. I needed a fix bad. Bill and I decided to satisfy our craving by going winter fly-fishing. The fishing season opens in New Hampshire on the first of January for ice-free rivers. As we arrived at the Newfound River, we could not believe the sight that greeted us. Cars parked all over, carrying license plates from New York, Vermont, Massachusetts, New Hampshire and Maine.

Bill and I fished the river a couple more times. We were better equipped on the following trips, adding wading staffs to our belts and fleece pants under our breathable waders. The last time we fished the river it started to snow. The snow clumped to the felt on the bottom of our waders as we hobbled back to the car. It was like walking with softballs tied to the underside of our feet. We were happy to take off the slippery waders, put away the rods, and watch the snow fall.

On the ride home we joked about the snowflakes resembling a large hatch of "White Millers." The "hatch" continued through the night. The next day the ground was white. The fly rods were put away and we went cross-country skiing, a much warmer sport than winter fly-fishing.

Opening Day

It was O-dark-thirty in the morning when the alarm sounded. I dressed, grabbed a cup of coffee, my fishing kit, and stole out of the house like a thief in the night. One hour before sunrise on the fourth Saturday of April is the opening of the New Hampshire trout pond season.

Driving north, through Franconia Notch, I noticed it had snowed during the night. Five inches of newly fallen snow covered the parking lot. Looking around, to my utter disbelief, I was completely alone in the dark. Usually, on opening day, the shores are lined with fishermen. It was not supposed to be this way.

I put on my waders, strung my rod, and started down the trackless path to Profile Lake. "Not a good sign, but I am here, so I may as well try it," I said to myself. I waded into the ice-cold water and worked line out through the frozen guides of my rod. The thermometer indicated a water temperature of thirty-four degrees. About a hitless hour later my hands were telling me to quit, my legs had stopped talking to me long ago. As the sun rose over Mount Lafayette, I reeled in my line and started up the still trackless path. April can be a cruel month and my fishing log recorded a cold, lonely, opening day.

The following year, applying lessons learned from the previous year, I waited for the sun to rise and headed south to try a different pond. There were half a dozen cars with fishermen standing around the parking lot. "Now this is a good sign," I said to myself as I gazed out over the still-gray pond. "Oh No," the reason the fishermen were standing around the still-gray pond was because it was ice covered.

One of the fishermen who had ventured out into the one small corner of the ice free water, cut his inflatable boat on the sharp ice edge and was packing his car to leave. As the sun rose higher over the trees, I could see the open water getting larger. Not one to quit, I decided to try fishing and waded into the water and cast my fly to the edge of the ice. As the sun rose higher and the open area continued to get larger the brook trout became active. The trout must have been concentrated in the open water as I had an active day of fishing shared by only a few other anglers. Next year, I may head further south searching for warmer open water on OPENING DAY. But I doubt I'll wait for the warmth to come to me.

Coffee

I heard the sloshing of coffee as the all-wheel drive Subaru Outback rolled over a large rock in the abandoned lumber road. I looked down at the insulated stainless steel Eddie Bauer coffee cup, the one I had given my wife years ago but have been using of late with her gracious permission. It was secure in its cup-holder. The sides of the roadway were lined with unfolding ferns and flowering shadbush.

Arriving at the end of the road, I parked the car and got out. A couple of red trillium caught my eye; they were scattered in among a group of white ones. I assembled my gear, inflated my float tube and attached a pair of carrying straps. I could hear a spring warbler of some kind singing as I started the walk to the pond. Maneuvering around blow downs was a little clumsy but I managed to reach the shore of the pond unharmed.

Solitude, sometime hard to find on larger bodies of water, greeted me. I had the whole pond to myself. Glancing around the shoreline, I took in the quiet beauty of the area. The still water reflected the budding trees and the blue sky. As I unhooked the carrying straps, I noticed a large dark shadow overhead; it was a turkey vulture that had just cleared the tree line and was now directly overhead, seemingly sizing me up, I must have looked healthy because the bird flew on.

I strapped on my kick-fins, put the float tube behind me and gently sat down. As I kicked away from shore, I hooked up the fishing apron. Secure in my little world I began searching for signs of trout. While rigging up I thought I saw a rise on the far shore, so I headed in that direction. As I worked my way over to the far shore (the far shore always seems better), I listened to a pileated woodpecker working on an old dead tree.

Brook trout would occasionally jump one to two feet out of the water attempting to catch the dragonflies and damselflies that were darting-about above the water. I attached a size 10 Cooper Bug that imitated a waterlogged dragonfly. The fly provided steady action. After kicking my way around the pond and with the sun low in the sky, I decided I had had enough enjoyment for one day. Walking out I noticed a moose print in the mud that had not been there when I walked into the pond. I glanced around to see if it was still in the area, but saw no further signs of the moose.

As I bumped my way over the rocks on the way out, coffee mug empty, all I could think about were the things I like about fishing. These are the kinds of memories that carry me through the fishless days of winter.

Too Much of a Good Thing

"Too many bait fish," I heard a fisherman grumble to his companion as they walked back to their car. I was standing in the water feeling thousands of one-inch-long menhaden bumping into my naked legs. Striped bass had herded the menhaden into the shallows and were slamming them into the balls of bait.

It was night-time and the darkness exaggerated the sounds and boils of the feeding bass. The moon was rising over my shoulder as I looked over and saw my fishing buddy, George, chasing a fish he had hooked. I went over to see if I could help, but George was able to beach the 33-inch long striper unassisted. The fish was well over the 28-inch minimum length limit and would make a great meal the next day. We continued to fish for another hour and decided to call it a night. George's striper was the only fish caught that night. It was clear the bass were after a mouthful of the 1-inch long menhaden and not interested in one single fly.

Our friends from Connecticut, George and Lori, invited Pat and me to their summer cottage in Charlestown, Rhode Island, to spend a couple of days. The plan was, George and I would fish and Pat and Lori would go looking for quilt shops.

George was new to fly-fishing and was anxious to try his new 11-weight rod. I, on the other hand, decided to try my 5-weight to make casting easier. We fished the Charlestown Breechway, a river-like connection between the ocean and an inland pond.

The next morning, no stripers were showing and the incoming tide was carrying weeds making it difficult to keep our flies clear of debris. George and I returned that evening to see the stripers starting to ball-up the menhaden and steer them into the shallows. I watched as some smaller fish were jumping two feet out of the water. I cast to them and got an immediate hook-up. I was surprised when the fish turned out to be shad. We caught a couple more shad before the stripers moved in.

In the dark, with the menhaden swimming against my legs, I continued fishing and watching the striper's feeding blitz. The stripers boiled all around me, and occasionally bump my legs—it was getting scary.

The moon was high in the sky when we realized all of the other fishermen had gone home and no one had caught any of the frenzied bass. George and I nodded to each other in the moonlight, "enough," and reeled in our lines and called it a night. Wading back to the car through all the baitfish, I shined the light into the water and thought that this must be what fish-jello would be like.

I have since been told, by experienced saltwater fishermen, the peanut bunker baitfish is the hardest to fish over. A fishermen dreams of stripers chasing baitfish, but on this trip I learned that there can be, too much of a good thing.

Willard Pond

Willard Pond is located in the dePierrefeu Willard Pond Wildlife Sanctuary, Antrim, New Hampshire. The pond covers 90-acres and lies in the shadow of Bald Mountain. It has a maximum depth of 58-feet, with an average depth of 30-feet. The shore is heavily wooded with only one camp house interrupting the wilderness forest. The water clarity is among the highest of New England lakes. Willard Pond is one of the few state waters containing tiger trout.

"Tiger" is descriptive not only of the color of this hybrid but of its disposition. The tiger trout is a cross between the female brown trout and the male brook trout. The progeny from this cross have tiger-like markings on their sides and are reportedly more aggressive than either parent species.

Angel and I decided to drive two hours to attempt catching one of these tiger trout. As we approached the launch area we could see several rising fish, always a good sign. We hastily rigged our gear and inflated the float tubes. As we kicked out to the rising fish we were impressed with the water clarity as we watched large boulders pass under us. No matter where we kicked, the risers always seemed to be out of casting range. Could it be due to the clear water?

As we fished, I watched several great blue herons working the shoreline for a late breakfast. I glanced over to Angel and saw his rod bent and a fish about three feet in the air. This first fish turned out to be a rainbow trout. An hour or so later I got my first strike. I set the hook to heavy resistance and worked the fish in to within about twenty feet of my float tube; the fish saw the tube and ran out all the line again. I worked him back and could see it was a large rainbow. I finally slipped the net under him and swung him onto my stripping apron. The lunker measured out to just over 18 inches, not bad on a #14 March Brown Spider. "This trip was worth it," I said to Angel as he took my picture with the prize rainbow trout. I released the beauty and we watched it slowly swim away.

Later in the day, I moved in closer to the rocks and was able to catch a half dozen 12 to 13-inch brook trout. This activity attracted a pair of loons that would swim under my tube, trying to relieve me of my catch. Go ahead and ask me if I like loons!

"No tiger trout today," I said to Angel as we decided to call it a day. It was a good day on the water. The hunt for "Tigers" will continue.

October Blitz

October, and the mountains are in full-parade-dress uniform. Brook trout are putting on their brilliant orange, black and white spawning colors. The larger male brook and brown trout develop their kype (hooked jaw). Fishermen are changing into thermals, fleece and wind-stopper fabrics. October fifteenth is the end of managed-trout pond season in New Hampshire. Angel and I plan on a fishing blitz, covering as many ponds as we can in the final two weeks of the season.

We started our last two weeks of fishing with a final try for pickerel on a fly. Having caught a couple of pickerel, I tied on a floating popper and cast it six inches from shore. It sat there for few seconds when something, ever so gently, sucked it in. It turned out to be a 5-pound smallmouth bass, an unexpected surprise.

The next day, we headed to Hildreth Dam to do some trout fishing; we each got a few brook and brown trout. A day later we went to Profile Lake where we encountered a flying-ant fall. The very next day, on a different pond, we again fished over flying-ants. Two days of great dry fly action for brook trout. I caught one a little over 17 inches and Angel got a 16-inch beauty. We fished Hall Pond, where we caught a couple of small brookies. I hiked into a remote pond and was rewarded with two brookies.

We took a road trip to Christine Lake in Stark, a neat little hamlet in The Great North Woods, but the wind was whipping the water into white caps, too dangerous for our float tubes. We broke out the topo-map to find an alternative place to fish. South Pond was nearby. The pond ran north/south and with the different orientation, was protected from the wind. We found it located in a beautiful recreation area, containing a beach and picnic area. I kicked my float tube into a shallow cove and found brook trout cruising in two feet of water. I had a ball sight fishing the flats.

On the way home, we stopped at Profile Lake for the last time. We had fished eight different ponds in twelve days during the last two weeks of the fishing season.

October's days are short and night comes early. With darkness approaching, we stepped out of the water and shook hands celebrating the end of our fishing blitz. As we walked to the car, after being in forty-six degree water for several hours, we begin to shiver. Driving home, with the car heater turned on high, we reminisced about the year and discussed future fishing adventures. It was time to put away the rods for the season; it was the end of our October blitz.

Grand Slam

Baseball's Grand Slam is hitting a home run with the bases loaded. Golf's Grand Slam is winning all four Majors in one year. Fishing's Grand Slam is catching several species of game fish in one day. For example, a salt water fishing grand slam would be catching a tarpon, bonefish and permit in the same day. Not an easy feat and is considered a rare achievement and may be a once in a lifetime occurrence.

One key factor to acquiring a grand slam is finding waters that contain several game fish. A lot of local trout water is home to only brook trout. Other waters contain brook and rainbow trout; not much of a challenge to catch one of each. Ponds and streams containing three or more species become more of a challenge.

But even if a body of water contains different species, each species has its own temperament and requirements. A brook trout prefers pockets in the cooler upper section of rivers while rainbows will be found in faster sections. Smallmouth bass prefer pools and back waters. Salmon live in the white water; water so fast you would not think a fish could swim there. Brown trout, the most elusive, prefer water with heavy cover near good feeding areas.

Hildreth Pond has produced grand slams of smallmouth bass, along with brook and brown trout, an interesting combination. Last year I caught brook trout, rainbow trout and brown trout in Russell Pond. This was amazing because the state only stocks brookies. I'm guessing a few rainbows and browns got mixed in by mistake.

The Androscoggin River is a real grand slam challenge as it holds all types of game fish. One day while fishing the Androscoggin, below the dam in Errol, I caught a couple of smallmouth bass, a brookie and rainbow trout. In the afternoon, I moved to the Thirteen Mile Woods section below Errol. Fishing a set of rapids I hooked and landed a land-locked salmon, "pretty good" I said to myself," four species." Later I moved below the rapids and managed to hook another fish. As I got the fish close enough to think about the net, I noticed the yellow-gold underbelly and distinctive red and black spots of a brown trout. I always considered the brown trout the most difficult to find and catch. I lifted the net, and indeed it contained a brown trout. That day I only landed seven fish but five were different species; a real GRAND SLAM.

Snook, Jacks & Tarpon

March is a month of waiting—waiting for the water to warm and the trout to become active. So, when Bob, a long-time friend of Bill's, invited us to come down to Cape Coral, Florida and do some saltwater fly-fishing, I jumped at the chance. The plan was Bill and I would fish with Bob, while the wives played golf, lie by the pool or just go gallivanting.

Arrival day, we fished locally around Sanibel, catching sea trout. The next day we went further afield, to the ten thousand-island area off the Everglades National Park. We edged our flats boat along the mangrove-lined shoreline tossing our flies under the overhanging branches. We were picking up an occasional snooklet (undersize snook, less than 27 inches) with a jack thrown in every now and then.

Bob spotted some surface activity in the middle of the lagoon. As we approached, Bob spotted a tarpon. I looked on in utter amazement at the largest fish I had ever seen. It was about six feet long. My friends handed me a 14-weight rod that seemed as stiff as a telephone pole. Bob said, "Now if you hook him, he will run for that point, but don't worry we will chase him with the boat." I looked at where he was pointing; it was a good mile away. "Do I need my passport?" I responded. Turned out I didn't' need it, because after about a dozen casts to the target, the tarpon spooked and shot out of sight.

The following day we cruised the flats around Captiva and Pine Island Sound looking for redfish. Bob managed to catch a shark and Bill got a nice snook. We did locate a school of redfish that were tucked in the mangroves. We had to cast our lines under the overhanging branches to catch them.

One night, after supper, we fished the canals for snook. A lot of boat docks have lights shining down into the water; these lights attract baitfish, which in turn attract snook.

It was a great week of fishing. We covered a lot of water, from the Everglades to Boca Grande. This was my first time fly-fishing for fish I had only read about. We caught snook, jack crevalle, redfish, sea trout, ladyfish and a shark.

Casting to that monster tarpon and night fishing for snook along the lighted docks was an experience I will remember for a long time.

Woolen Winters of Yore

I am often asked if I ice-fish. The simple answer is, No—but I did a lot as a youth and young adult. I came from a fishing family, my father, uncles and cousins all fished year round. In the summer we fished for trout and in the winter we fished for pickerel and yellow perch. In those days you could not legally fish for trout through the ice, a policy I agree with to this day. I think it is a waste of a beautiful game fish to be caught on a hand line.

Pickerel fishing was primarily done using traps, no bob-house in my past. Now a trap, for you who don't know what they are, are a wooden frame with a reel at one end, a spring-loaded flag at the other end and a cross piece in the center to prevented the trap from falling through. A hole, about 8 inches in diameter, was chopped in the ice using a homemade ice chisel; again this was before power augers. The hook was baited with a minnow and the trap was placed in the hole with the reel in the water to prevent freezing. When a fish took the bait the flag was tripped and would pop up.

Perch fishing was best done with a jig. Jigging consisted of a short rod and a baited jig-like lure. The lure was jigged up and down and the flash attracted near-by fish. It was common to cut over a hundred holes in search of a school of perch.

I wore wool; the miracle fabrics of today were not available. I started with long woolen (itchy) underwear covered with a woolen shirt and red plaid Woolrich hunting pants about an inch thick.

Over all this, I topped it off with a sheepskin-lined brown canvas, knee length, mutton-collared coat my grandfather brought over from Poland. Woolen hat, leather insulated gloves and insulated rubber boots completed the outfit. All these clothes weighed a ton. When I took them off, at the end of the day, I felt as though I were floating.

My father and uncle wore army-surplus, alpaca-lined hooded coats that were worn during the Korean War.

Although ice fishing equipment and methods (synthetic-fiber clothing, power ice augurs, GPS locators, fish finders and underwater video cameras) has improved, I now prefer cross-country skiing and snowshoeing to ice fishing.

Close Encounters

The blurred-brown movement contrasted against the white snow covered ground. I had stopped to assess a steep-downhill section of a Bretton Woods cross-country ski trail. I was enjoying a tour through the snow-covered forest. Since I stopped ice fishing, Nordic skiing became one of my favorite winter activities. It keeps me outdoors and presents opportunities to see wildlife. On rare occasion, I not only see wildlife but also make contact at some level.

As I stood there trying to determine the direction of the twisting downhill section of the trail, I saw the blurred-brown movement out of the corner of my eye. I turned my head and watched an American (Pine) marten approach me. He seemed deep in thought, and not aware that I was there. The marten got to about twenty feet of me before he became aware of my presence. He stopped, and we both looked at each other for a long time. "This is great—I had never seen a marten this close before," I though. The marten seemed to be thinking, "What is this big black thing—it's in my way—how can I get around it?" Finally, the marten walked around me and continued on his way, thinking whatever it is that martens think about when the are walking through the woods.

Another close encounter, only on a much larger scale, occurred on a Waterville Valley ski trail, appropriately named Moose Run. I came around a sharp bend and found myself face to face with a large moose. I slammed on the brakes and stopped as fast as could. As I watched the moose, I became aware that it was not alone; there were three others just off the trail. I was surrounded by them. I watched for a while hoping they would move off. The moose looked down their nose at me and continued grazing. Realizing they were not going to move, I did a step turn and slowly skied away, all the while looking over my shoulder.

On an annual trip to the Balsam's Wilderness, I had my closest encounter. Two birds flew across the trail and landed on a mid-height branch. I stopped to identify them and recognized them as gray jays. My first encounter with this species was in Wyoming, on a cross-country road trip. My wife and I were enjoying a picnic lunch, when a pair of these "camp robbers" flew down and helped themselves to our grapes.

I watched the two birds for a while; finally I held out my hand and extended my finger for a perch, and made a soft clicking sound. To my amazement one of the jays flew off the branch and landed on my finger. Realizing there was no food, he flew off. The second jay flew to my finger and checked my finger for himself.

This, I think, is as close as an encounter with wildlife as one can expect.

Snowshoe Hare's Ear

The winter was long (snow covering the ground since the beginning of December) and cold (with temperatures seldom reaching the freezing mark and nights well below zero). The first warm days of March got this old man's fancy turning to, you guessed it, FISHING. I could hear the trout calling as soon as the river showed itself from below the ice and snow.

The dilemma was where to go fishing. Ponds were ice covered, the streams protected by a couple of feet of snow. SNOWSHOES! Why not combine two of my favorite sports and snowshoe into a brook and fish a couple of nice pools I found last summer.

I dug out my fishing gear and picked out a few flies to take along. Bead head nymphs and wet flies were my first choice, which to me meant a Hare's Ear and a soft hackle Spider. A Rat Faced McDougal was thrown in, just in case trout were rising. I decided to go light because I figured I would be doing more snowshoeing than fishing.

F-Day came, rivers finally free of ice, sun shining and temperatures in the forties. I drove out and parked the car at the trailhead. I put on my hip boots and strapped on my snowshoes. I started out on a packed hiking trail, and shortly turned into the forest and headed toward the stream. The snowshoeing was much more difficult off the hiking trail, sinking in the soft corn snow to over my knees. Bushwhacking in hip-boots and carrying a fly rod was much more challenging than the pleasant snowshoe hikes I experienced when only snowshoeing.

Upon reaching the river, I took off my snowshoes, tied on a Hare's Ear nymph and stepped into the stream. The water temperature was a cold thirty-five degrees. I cast to the head of the pool and watched my line for any signs of a hit. Nothing. After about twenty hitless-minutes, I hiked up-stream to a couple of other pools, same thing. Apparently the trout were not as enthusiastic to get the season started as I was.

Climbing out of the water onto the bank, I observed a chewed down sapling, indicating working beavers. Hiking out I noticed fresh bear tracks heading toward town, down the same path I just came up. The bear's huge tracks neatly overlaid my snow shoe tracks. Making as much noise as I could, I pushed along, hoping the bear was walking faster than I was. As I watched for the black bear, I noticed several tracks crossing the trail. The tracks were of Snowshoe Hares.

Chalk Streams

Maps arrived in February. Size 8 and 10 Green Drake dry flies were tied in March—all part of planning and preparation for fishing central Pennsylvania's fabled chalk streams. Angel and I made reservations to fish with Rocco Rosamilia, of Keystone Anglers, located in Lock Haven, Pennsylvania; we wanted to try our hand at some classic dry fly fishing.

The classic dry fly streams are the chalk streams of England, the limestone streams of Pennsylvania and the spring creeks of the west. The classic dry fly fish is the brown trout. They hold steady just under the surface selectively picking off insects washed-down to them by the rivers current. If a brown trout is to be fooled into hitting, the fly must be precisely placed and float drag-free in the feeding lane directly to the fish. We wanted to see if we were up to the challenge.

The first day we fished White Deer Creek, a mountain freestone stream about 20 to 30-feet across, containing a mixture of pools and runs. I fished a March Brown dry fly and a lime green inchworm imitation as the dropper. Working my way upstream I was able to fool several brown trout and a few brookies.

Wanting to sample various waters, we moved to Long Run Creek. I came upon a tree that had fallen in the water, and remembering my father's instructions about LWD, assessed the situation. A nest of branches prevented me from casting to the main trunk. Just then Rocco walked up behind me. I explained the situation and he confirmed my thought, throw the fly in the woodpile and hope for the best. I placed the fly in the pocket and a fish hit as soon as the fly landed. Somehow I managed to work the fish out of the large woody debris and land a golden-colored wild brown trout.

Next, Rocco took us to the headwaters of Fishing Creek, a classic spring creek. This creek was about 15-feet across and flowed through a meadow with dairy cows on both sides. The cows did not seem to mind sharing their meadow and even escorted me to the water. The banks had brush on both sides, so again I fished straight upstream to avoid the bushes. Angel and I were able to land several nice brook trout with a few brownies thrown in for good measure. We decided to catch the evening hatch downstream on the Fishing Creek. We stopped and got three hoagies and drinks, drove to the water and ate our supper as we watched for mayflies and risers.

The following day we drove north to the freestone flow of Young Women's Creek. Unlike the milky, chalky color of the limestone creeks, these creeks flowed clear. Again the conditions were favorable and the fishing good. The creeks were easy to wade and the forest was cleared of underbrush by the many deer that inhabit the area.

For the evening hatch, Rocco suggested we hit a larger creek. We packed up and headed for Kettle Creek.

Kettle Creek

Kettle Creek was wide, 200-feet across, much larger than any creeks we had fished up to now. Rocco told us we would try the tailwaters below Alvin Bush Dam. We parked, had our supper and watched for insects and risers. We saw a few risers, and Angel and I fished over them.

Rocco suggested we drive downstream and try another spot before dark. We parked and Rocco told Angel to try downstream and he and I would walk upstream. As we walked, we could see a dozen or so trout working on a hatch of sulfurs (mayflies). I stepped into the water and slowly approached the pod of trout. Rocco determined they were sipping emergers. Emergers are the stage of a mayfly when the nymph swims to the surface, shed their outer-case, and hatch as adult mayfly duns. I switched to a size 16 sulfur emerger fished on 6x (.005" dia.) tippet. This type of fly is designed to float in the surface-film, very hard for the angler to see. I cast and watched a brown rise up, follow my fly downstream, turn upside-down and sip in the fly. I called Angel to join us. We continued to catch fish as the trout continued sipping the emergers.

As the sun set, it got more and more difficult to see the tiny floating emergers. I shortened my cast to compensate for the darkness. Angel and Rocco were about a hundred feet upstream and I could hear Rocco talking to Angel. It was like listening to a guide talking to a blind person. The conversation went something like this, "your long—a little shorter—cast to the right—he's coming—he's coming—PULL!" and then I would hear the splash of a fish resisting capture. Rocco's twenty-four-year-old eyes were that much better than ours. About 10:00 pm, it was so dark even Rocco's young eyes could not see the fly. We fished another half-hour and caught a couple more browns on pure instinct.

Fishing Pennsylvania's spring creeks was everything we had hoped it would be, classic dry fly-fishing, for brown trout. Best of all, Angel and I proved we were up to the challenge of catching the wily brown trout. Rocco was a great guide and made us feel at home, and as Pennsylvania's license plate wrote "you have a friend in Pennsylvania."

Dick Talleur wrote in his book, *Dry-Fly Handbook,* "If an angel were to come down from above and say to me, 'Listen; we've decided you can fish every day for the rest of your life, but only one way, and on one kind of water. What's your choice?' I'd reply without hesitation, I'll take dry fly-fishing on a spring creek."

A River Runs By It

Everyone who has seen the movie, *A River Runs Through It,* remembers the scene where the protagonist is standing in the river casting a fly. The line shimmering in the late-day sun, traveling back and forth, in perfect loops, shooting out 80 or 90-feet. Beautiful? Yes. Inspiring? Definitely. Realistic? I don't think so.

The movie prompts most newcomers to fly-fishing to ask for casting lessons. "Keep your head down—your left arm straight—eye on the ball" are directions you would hear during a golf lesson. Try thinking about all those instructions at once and you are lucky to hit the ball at all. "10 o'clock to 2 o'clock—elbow tight to side—keep your wrist stiff—thumb on top of grip" are fly casting instruction that have the same results—mind clutter. What the newcomers should be asking for is fishing lessons, where they would learn the advantage of fishing a short line.

Beginners want to learn to cast a mile, while experienced fly fishermen will work as short a line as he can. I remember watching an old-timer dapping a fly in Tim Pond, Maine. Fishing from a Maine Grand Lake canoe, using line only the length of his rod, he flipped his fly out and skated it across the surface. Brookies rose from the depths and took his fly 10 feet from the boat. He got as many strikes per cast as the longest casters.

It's fun to be able to cast out the entire line and a long cast is nice to have in your arsenal. But if you want to learn how to cast, practice casts that will be useful on the water. Practice casting to a target, or curved casts bending the line around rocks and obstacles. Practice putting slack in the line on a downstream cast in order to float a drag free dry fly. A side arm cast to place a fly under overhanging trees can come in handy. This type of casting will produce many more hits than long casts.

To cast a long line while fishing a pond may be helpful. I find that even in this case a really long cast is not always practical. Fish will often hit shortly after the fly lands on the water. With all the slack in the line it is very hard to feel a hit or set the hook. Often I will shorten my cast to better observe trout rising to a fly.

The more false casting done by the angler, the longer the fly is in the air. False casting is good for birds not fish. Fishing begins when the lure hits the water. The more time the fly is in the water, the more time you're actually fishing, air time doesn't count. When you're on the water, continue to remind yourself you are fishing not casting. Remember the beautiful images from *A River Runs Through It*, but keep in mind that it is not an instructional film.

Everything Happens at Once

Early morning on Profile Lake and I am alone on the pond. I'm slowly kicking my way up the shoreline, casting a Special K streamer and slowly retrieving it. I am looking up at the majestic mountains, looking at the remains of the Old Man of the Mountains, looking at the Old Lady of the Mountains, enjoying the solitude. It is quiet, except for the cars and trucks rushing by on the Franconia Notch Parkway.

Spinning the tube around to see where I'm going, I look up the shore and spot what first looked like a yellow Labrador retriever, frolicking in the water along the shore. With closer observation, I determine it's a deer. The sun is reflecting off the doe's tan hide. I am amazed to see a deer in the rugged terrain of Franconia Notch. The doe is enjoying the sun-lit morning by, stiff-leg jumping, running and splashing in the water. Not the least bit afraid or concerned with my approach.

As I get closer, I begin to think about digging the camera out of my vest. I am now fully concentrated on watching the doe playing in the water. Something pulls my line. "Oh no, not now, I want to take a picture of the deer," I think to myself. The pull gets stronger and gets my notice. I look at my rod and it's bent in half and the fish is running line out. The fish now has my complete attention. As I fight the fish, I try to keep one eye on the deer. Finally the fish is in sight, it's enormous. A "Walter," if ever I saw one.

I get the huge fish on the stripping apron of my float tube. The fish lies there covering the apron, waiting for its picture to be taken. The deer is now standing still, watching what I am doing. The camera is still buried in my vest. As I begin to dig it out to get a picture of the monster, the fish gets tired of waiting and jumps off the apron. The fish is gone, but now I have the camera out. I take a quick picture of the deer standing in the water and start kicking myself closer to the deer. As I advance the film to get a better picture of the deer splashing along the shore, the film comes to the end of the roll. Everything seems to be happening at once.

The deer waves its ears at me and slowly walks into the woods. It is in the area between the pond and Rt. 93. I worry about the deer crossing the road. No change in the sound of traffic; that's good. A couple of hours later the deer walks out of the trees for a cooling drink of water. It must have bedded down in the island of trees. She is safe for now. The monster trout is also safe. I wish them both a long life.

Evening Hatch

Summertime—and the hatches are easy. Fish are jumping—but not in the day. It was a hot, still, summer day and my wife was going to go out with the girls. It was a good time to fish the evening hatch at Profile Lake. Profile Lake has the reputation of being an "evening pond," with late-evening hatches along with rising trout. The fishing regulations allow fishing for brook trout up to two hours after sunset. I got there about 4:00 pm, a little early, but I thought I would try fishing deep with a sinking line. As I rigged up, I could see some dimples on the still water. Looked promising.

I launched my float tube and kicked toward deeper water. On my second cast I felt a slight resistance and set the hook. It was a 4-inch yellow perch, explaining the dimples I had seen. I thought it had been too good to be true. My first trout didn't come until an hour and a half later. "Oh Good," I thought, "Things will pick up now." After another hitless hour, I decided to switch to a floating line and try some dry flies. Although there were no bugs on the surface, I figured I had nothing to lose and it certainly would be more fun. Shortly a brook trout rose and took my fly. "Here we go," I said to myself. But again this was followed by a long hitless period.

Since it was getting dark and I had been fishing for well over four hours, I decided to throw in the towel. There were only a few insects showing, although I had seen one large mayfly that had been quickly taken by a trout. As I was kicking my way back to shore, a boat with a father and daughter were rowing out. He informed me; he was there the day before and had caught a half dozen fish, all after 8:30 pm. Since it was almost that time, I figured I might as well stay a little longer.

About fifteen minutes later, a trout rose about thirty feet from me. I cast to the rise and the fly was immediately sucked in. For the next fifteen minutes, no matter where I cast, I was fast to a squaretail. It was as if someone rang the dinner bell. Unfortunately darkness had set in and the bats were out in strength, zooming just above my head. I shortened my cast, hoping it would compensate for not being able to see the end of my rod. At the sound of a splash, in the vicinity of my fly, I quickly set the hook hoping the trout was after my fly. I decided I had enough fun and it was time to quit. I kicked my way back to the boat-landing half heartedly casting a short line and getting hits—I think. After over five hours of fishing, I had caught, all but two, of the fish in the last half an hour.

This trip was typical of fishing the evening hatch, reminding me of a baseball game. Full of anticipation with all the excitement crammed into a short time. The evening fishing will always have a fascination, because of the potential of getting into that magical feeding frenzy of an evening hatch.

On the Road Again

Whenever I'm in Bristol, New Hampshire, I stop in Charlie's Fly-tying shop. I stop not only to add more feathers to my fly tying stash, but also to chat with Charlie Poole about fishing. In one of our discussions, Charlie mentioned that he used to fish two trout ponds in Loudon New Hampshire, Clough Pond and Hot Hole Pond. When I got home I looked at a map of Loudon and discovered that the two ponds were near one another. Seeing how my fishing partner and I like to try new ponds, it was time to hit the road again.

We decided to fish Clough Pond first, because it was the larger of the two ponds and held the most promise. Clough Pond covers 46-acres and has a of 57-foot maximum depth. The pond is surrounded with homes and summer cottages with a nice public access boat ramp on the eastern shore. While we were inflating our float tubes, the Loudon Fire Department drove in with their Rescue Boat. "Hope you are not here to rescue us," I said, but they answered they were there to set the floats for the town beach and were sure their expertise would not be needed.

I fished the shoreline and a shallow rocky bar in the center of the pond. A couple of hours later all I had caught were a few golden shiners and a couple of sunfish. I tried to fish the drop-off along the shore but due to low water clarity, could not see the bottom. After fishing three quarters of the shoreline, it was time to try the next pond. As I stated kicking back, a trout rose near me. I cast to the rise and a brookie took the fly.

Hot Hole Pond is smaller, at 27-acres and 42-feet deep. There is a boat launch at the western end of the pond. Adjacent to the access ramp is a handicap fishing platform, along with nearby handicap parking. Several fishermen were enjoying the platform on this day. Both ponds provided rest room facilities. Loudon certainly treats its residents and guests well.

As I kicked away from the launch area, I saw a large fish jump out of the water close to shore. As I watched the rings disappear my 3-weight rod doubled over. A 2-pound largemouth bass inhaled my fly, a great start.

I had a blast fishing the shoreline catching bass. I decided to move out to deeper water and try for trout. A friendly passing boater, with a fish finder, told me that the trout were down at the 22-foot level, too deep to reach fly-fishing.

I went back to the shallow water and tied on a Zoo Cougar to finish the day fishing for bass. At the end of the day, as I approached the takeout point, a huge bass smashed the Zoo Cougar and jumped out of the water. I estimated the bass to be in the 20-inch range. Since I had not changed from my 4x trout leader to a more substantial bass leader, the bass broke off on the second jump.

These stories are why I enjoy trips to new waters, never knowing what will happen, whom you will meet, or how the fishing will be. Certainly, it will not be long before I go on the road again.

Grand Lake Stream

One must drive through the Passamaquoddy Indian Reservation to get to the sporting camps in the village of Grand Lake Stream, located in eastern Maine, northwest of Eastport, near the St Croix River, bordering New Brunswick, Canada. For several years my father and I would return for a week or so for some exhilarating fishing.

I have many fond memories of the time my dad and I spent together. We would fish West Grand Lake for salmon and trout. Back in those days land-locked salmon in the 5 to 8-pound range were common. Big Lake provided some fine smallmouth bass fishing with bass up to 5-pounds. We spent a day or two fishing the smaller ponds. Wabassus Lake gave up some fine smallmouth bass and white perch. The Machias chain of lakes and its thoroughfares provide spectacular pickerel fishing; pickerel over 25-inches were common.

Often, after supper, I would walk down to Grand Lake Stream and try my hand at catching a salmon on a fly. I was, at that time, just learning to fly fish and had little experience stream fishing. I would wade in just below the logging dam and cast into the river hoping for something to happen.

One evening I convinced my dad to get a picture of me casting in the river. He was familiar with basic cameras but my single-lens reflex camera overwhelmed him. I selected a spot on the shore and framed the scene and set the exposure, handing him the camera I explained my plan. I would walk to the other side of the river and cast toward the camera. Walter was to look through the viewfinder and push the button when a cast looked good.

I walked to the other side of the river and waded in and started casting. I saw my father fumbling with the camera. I stopped casting and my line fell to the water. Over the sound of the river, I shouted the instructions again. Walter slowly raised the camera and pushed the button.

Just as he snapped the picture, in that split-second, a salmon smacked my fly and shot into air, I raised my rod to set the hook. A moment in time caught on film, and in a young boy's mind forever.

Pickerel

The orange and white foam-popping bug hit the water with a SPLAT. On the second twitch a wash-tub size swirl appeared under the fly. The fish and I failed to accomplish hook-up. I cast to the same spot, same swirl, same miss. On the third cast I made the popper—POP. A pickerel the size of an Ohio Class submarine inhaled the fly, the rod bent in half as I began a long fight.

Shortly before my fly was attacked, I heard my fishing companion, hooting and hollering. His rod bent double as a super-sized pickerel was towing his float tube around. I watched as he carefully reached down and lifted the fish onto the float tube's stripping apron. Later he told me a quarter of the pickerel overhung the 18-inch long ruler imprinted on the apron.

Pickerel are the smallest member of the pike family and are the fresh water equivalent of a barracuda. Like their older brother, the pike, they have a mouth loaded with rows of razor sharp teeth. They tend to hide in aquatic plants and assassinate prey as they swim by. They have been known to attack young ducks. Their strike is vicious, sometime attacking from a distance of 10 to 20-feet. Pickerel attack from the side, killing their prey before turning it around to swallow it headfirst.

I had been chasing the elusive pickerel in various ponds for the last couple of years. The past trips were always in August, when the trout fishing slowed and the trout were deep. My fishing buddy and I floated many ponds catching mostly chubs and pan fish on our huge pickerel flies. Occasionally I hooked and landed a hammer-handle size pickerel.

Acting on a hot tip, I decided to try for pickerel once again. This trip was late September, after the water-cooled down. Prime trout time, but I really wanted to catch some respectable pickerel.

In preparation for the trip I had tied some 4-inch long Mickey Finns and a few oversized chartreuse Zonkers. My tapered trout leaders were replaced with level 25-pound test monofilament leaders tipped with 5-inch wire leaders. On past trips, I felt a bump only to bring in a line with no fly attached. With one bite, the pickerel simply bit the fly off.

This September trip was wildly successful. The colder water seemed to have made the difference. My large flies were attacked and slashed with vicious violence by oversized pickerel.

Le Grand Bois Du Nord

"Le Grand Bois Du Nord," the sign whizzed by as Angel and I drove toward our fishing destination. I had fished "The Great North Woods" of New Hampshire many times before, but always used Errol or Pittsburg as the center of operations. On this trip we planned to fish ponds in and around Colebrook, ponds that we had never fished before.

Angel and I were on another end of the season fishing trip. Filled with excitement, we pulled into the parking lot of our first target, Fish Pond in Columbia. It's a small, 30-acre, shallow, 8-foot maximum depth, pond. The water was perfectly still, reflecting the autumnal colors of the local flora. The morning's fishing produced several largemouth bass. Over the next few days, every time we mentioned fishing Fish Pond, people replied, "Oh you must have caught some bass." Obviously it's a spring trout fishery.

That afternoon we drove to Little Diamond Pond. A Forest Ranger told us that the water had cooled down and the trout were biting. He also told us about some local remote ponds that were worth fishing. We launched our tubes and within 15 minutes I had caught 3 brook trout. Angel kicked close to me, nodding this was going to be a great afternoon. But three hours later, Angel had caught one fish and I caught another squaretail—one never knows.

We checked into the Colebrook House and Inn, late Monday evening. The new owners, recently relocated from Colorado, informed us the restaurant and lounge were closed on Mondays and Tuesdays. As our room was directly over the bar, the fact that the bar was closed did not upset us. We crossed the street to Howard's Restaurant where I had a nice turkey dinner and Angel had chicken parmigiana. Morning found us back at Howard's for breakfast. The owner, told us the restaurant dates back to 1858, and being the gateway to Dixville Notch (the first in the nation to vote) many presidents and presidential candidates have graced Howard's. Across the street, we visited the well equipped Ducret's Sporting Goods, for some last minute fishing supplies and local knowledge.

Next, we were off to fish one of the remote ponds the Forest Ranger told us about. The morning was spent finding and exploring the pond. The fishing was productive, so we decided to spend the afternoon on the pond. After an hour-long lunch break, we resumed fishing. To our pleasure we discovered the trout quite active. We not only caught a lot more fish, but much larger fish. Once the brookies reached 14 inches and more, they really grew in girth. These larger squaretails began to resemble footballs.

The last pond we fished was Mirror Lake. Angel kicked out to the middle of the cove and I kicked along the shoreline. Several trout porpoised nearby and eagerly hit my fly—3 casts, 3 fish. I called to my partner who kicked over to join me. Angel and I spent the next couple of hours catching and releasing trout after trout ranging in size from 12 to 16-inches in length.

This would be our last road trip of the season. The weather was summer-like, the accommodations were friendly and pleasant, the foliage was at its peak color and the fish were colorful and plentiful. We were treated very well in Le Grand Bois Du Nord.

Acorns

"Even a blind squirrel finds an acorn every now and then,"—a proverb we have all heard one time or another. I think this is wonderful way of saying, "sometime it's just dumb luck." Sometimes, fishermen can find acorns.

One of the first acorns I found, I found on Cape Cod while my wife and I were celebrating her mother's August birthday. I found some free time in the middle of the day and decided to go fishing. It was a hot humid August day and I figured all the trout would be near the bottom in the cooler water. I selected a two-tiered pond, a pond with both coldwater and warmwater fish. Herring Pond was one of those ponds. It contained trout, bass and perch and I was sure I could catch some perch and maybe even a bass.

I parked the car and walked toward the pond. The shore was a typical cape pond with a sandy shallow bar going out 100 or more feet. I strung my line and tied on a Black-Nosed Dace, all the while thinking I may not even be able to catch a perch in 80° water. People were swimming and splashing along the sandy shore, further reducing my potential success. "Oh well," I said to myself, "it's a nice day and I'm here, so I might as well try it."

I started wading out toward deeper water, working the line out by roll casting my streamer out ahead of me. In ankle deep crystal-clear water my line suddenly stopped short. I tried to roll cast the line again but the end remained fixed. I stripped in the excess line and discovered I had a fish on the end of my line. It turned out to be a rainbow trout, one of the largest fish of the season.

Another acorn was found on the Mad River while I was fishing with a close friend. Bill was fairly new to fly-fishing at the time. For over an hour, he worked a pool he was convinced held trout. I stood and watched him fish the pool for a while. Finally, Bill was ready to give up and move on.

"Bill," I said, "let me show you how to mend the line in order to get a better drift."

He handed me his rod; I cast to the center of the pool and said, "Bill, if you mend your line by flipping some line upstream, it will create slack giving you a drag-free drift." As I talked, I threw an upstream mend in the line. The fly floated perfectly down the center of the pool.

We watched the fly bounce along down the center of the pool, and suddenly, a beautiful brook trout rose from the bottom and sucked in Bill's Humpy. I instinctively set the hook. Realizing I had Bill's rod, I quickly handed the rod back to him with some embarrassment.

I found another acorn that day; it was on that day Bill nicknamed me, "The Professor."

Nine in a Row

The sun was shining brightly one calm, spring morning. A friend and I decided to fish Russell Pond in hope of hitting the mid-day hatches the pond was known for. Fred, a longtime fly fisherman, and I lashed the canoe to the roof of his car. Beth, Fred's wife, came out of the house and watched us finish loading our gear and waved us off, wishing us luck.

Upon arriving at the pond, we could see some trout working along the northern shoreline. We unloaded the canoe, strung our rods and pushed off. I told Fred to get ready as I paddled us slowly and stealthily into position and dropped anchor. I positioned the canoe in about fifteen feet of water, a hundred feet from shore. We could see bottom in the crystal-clear water and watched trout as they cruised along the shore picking off caddis flies as they swam along.

Fred cast his Hornberg; the fly landed softly on the water and gently floated on the surface. We watched a brookie rise from the depths and smack the fly. Fred set the hook and was fast to the first fish of the day. This scene was repeated again and again. Fred had had nine brook trout rise to his fly and brought nine to net. Fred hooked and landed nine consecutive trout, must be some kind of record, certainly one of the best hook-up rates I have witnessed. The next fish that rolled over Fred's fly missed, breaking his streak of hook-ups.

Let me explain, it's not easy catching trout on a still water dry fly. Set the hook too quick and you pull the fly away, too slow and it's spit out. Sometime the trout detect the imitation and turn away or they just plain miss the fly.

It was an incredible morning of fishing. Now, about noontime, we had fished our way a quarter of the way around the pond. I asked Fred how long he wanted to stay and he agreed we were having way too much fun to even think about leaving. I asked if he had brought a lunch, he responded that he had not. I offered him one of the Power Bars that I always carry in my vest, and a drink of water, all I had to offer.

A couple hours later we had slowly worked our way back to the take-out point on the shore. At that time we decided we had had enough fun for one day. As we drove into Fred's yard and began unloading the canoe, Beth came out to greet us. She remarked that it was late afternoon and asked if we had lunch. Fred told her we were enjoying ourselves too much to stop fishing and had lost track of time. Beth was concerned about Fred not having a proper lunch,

It was then I realized I am not a very good guide, only providing a Power Bar and water. Fred told me later, that this was the best day of fishing he had in a long time, and couldn't have cared less about lunch at the time, and he would definitely go fishing with me again. Nine-in-a-row is as good as lunch any day.

Rapid River

The Rapid River runs through the historically rich wilds of Maine, from Richardson Lake 3.2 miles to Lake Umbagog. The region is largely the same as it was then and still contains the same strain of wild brook trout.

Pat, a fly-fishing friend, who is very familiar with the area, offered to guide my fishing companion, Angel, and me for a day of fishing. She gave us detailed direction to navigate the fifteen miles of dirt roads to the first gate. The road to the river is gated, with limited access. She met us at the gate and drove us the two miles to the river itself.

Pat gave us a quick tour of the camp and the surrounding area. She told us that in 1985 someone illegally stocked smallmouth bass in Lake Umbagog and the bass were working themselves up river, threatening the native brook trout population. She asked us to please kill any bass we caught.

We suited up and hiked to the river. The first stop on the tour was the famous Lower Dam. We each selected a spot and began casting with the hope of catching one of the fabled five-pound Rapid River wild brook trout. No luck, but Pat did catch a salmon and Angel got a nice brookie. All fish were quickly released, this is a catch and release fishery.

Pat then took us to the Long Pool to try our luck there and to show us the river. Next we went to Smooth Ledge Pool, again to fish and tour the river. Our next stop was the well-known Pond-in-the-River.

It was the last week of Maine's trout fishing season, the last chance to catch a trophy trout. Even at that I was surprised to see as many anglers as we did. Thinking back to the fifteen miles of dirt roads, plus a three-mile hike, they were certainly motivated.

Our last stop was a hike to the Middle Dam. It was late evening and I was dog-tired, but we fished this last area. Pat had done a wonderful job of showing us the river. We did not manage to catch one of the trophy brookies the Rapid River is famous for, but we had an opportunity to cast classic flies on a classic river.

It was dark by the time Angel and I headed out. I was careful to note all the forks in the road, the twists and turns and mileages on the way in. After multiple turns, with the bushes rubbing the car on both sides, Angel and I looked at each other and agreed the road did not look this narrow on the way in. Did we follow the directions and my notes properly? Were we lost? A little bit of panic set in—thoughts of spending the night in the car eating Power Bars and drinking water for supper. We suddenly came to Rt. 16 exactly where we turned in. Things surely look different at night. We turned left toward our lodging, the Magalloway Inn—but that's another story.

Magalloway Inn

Angel and I were fishing the Rapid River and other classic rivers in Maine's historic Rangeley area. The area is well known for its brook trout and landlocked salmon fishing. This is the area where Carrie Stevens tied the first Gray Ghost and changed streamer fly patterns forever. This area produced some of the most famous hackle streamers, the Nine-Three, Supervisor, and Black Ghost, along with one of the prettiest wet flies, e.g., the white-and-scarlet married wing of the Parmachene Belle.

We had selected the Magalloway Inn/Mt. Dunstan Cabins, located on Rt. 16 in Wentworth Location, New Hampshire, as our base camp. The B&B would provide us a breakfast to start our long day of fishing with a full stomach. After a hardy breakfast we drove north and crossed the Maine line. Our target for the day was the nearby Magalloway River. We hiked down to the river and agreed that I would hike upstream and fish down while Angel fished the big pool.

I fished my way back to the pool and found Angel sitting on a rock waiting to tell me a couple of stories. He told me, he hooked this huge fish and fought it for several minutes before realizing he had hooked a rock. Later, moving to another spot he slipped and landed on his rod, breaking it into two pieces. The rod was guaranteed but would not be replaced until he returned to Massachusetts. He was going to drive to Errol and get another rod at L.L. Cote. I recommended that he buy a lighter 3-weight outfit to replace his broken 5-weight, preventing owning two 5-weight rods.

That night we stopped at the nearby Mt. Dunstan Country Store next to the Inn for some supper. I ordered an Italian Sub sandwich. I watched as she cut the bread and started to fill it with lettuce and tomatoes. She went on to lay three layers of cheese topped with what looked like 5 pounds of various cold cuts. I was charged some ridiculously low price for this sandwich and a drink. Back at the Magalloway Inn, I could not close the sandwich because of the amount of meat, and ate it as an open face sandwich.

The next day we fished the Steep Bank Pool on the Kennebago River. It wasn't long before a large salmon ate Angel's Pheasant Tail nymph. The salmon bent Angel's new 3-weight rod in half. He called for some help, as he forgot his net. I walked up and looked at the fish. I told Angel it looked too big to fit in my trout net and he was better off beaching it. Angel was not familiar with this technique; eventually I was able to get the salmon's head and front half of his body into my small net. It was one of the widest salmon I had ever seen.

Back at the Magalloway Inn, we enjoyed a huge piece of Lasagna we had purchased for a pittance at the general store. After three days of fishing rivers we slept like babies. This trip will long be remembered for Angel's huge salmon, the meals at the Mt. Dunstan Country Store and the hospitality of the Magalloway Inn.

27 Degrees

27 degrees! 27 degrees? That's what I saw on the thermometer as I shut off the ringing of the alarm clock. The previous few weeks were unseasonably warm and I was quickly spoiled with the thoughts of spring, but this was opening day of fishing in ponds managed for trout. Traditionally, opening day is cold, but this caught me by surprise. I decided to have a leisurely cup of coffee and let things warm up a bit. When the temperature finally reached the upper thirties, I drove to the pond. Fishermen were starting to come off the water, stiff from the cold.

I tied on one of my favorite early season flies, the Special K, (one of my own designs), and began casting. After only a few casts, a brook trout rose and nailed my fly. I found the fish cooperative that day. They were located close to shore, where the water was a little warmer.

This was not my first trip of the year. I always go out on a shake-down cruise before the regular trout season opens. Ponds that are not managed for trout are open for fishing. I like to check out my equipment, making sure my waders and float tube don't leak. This shake-down cruise was a success. Not only did all my gear perform as required, but I caught two brown trout, one of which was a lunker.

The next day, Sunday, was a little warmer but raining. About 9 o'clock, it stopped raining and I decided to give it a go. When I arrived at the pond, my car thermometer registered 40 degrees.

As I suited up, it began to rain, but once in my waders and rain jacket, I am sealed in and can stay dry, maybe not warm but dry. As I fished the shoreline the rain began to bounce off the water and off my jacket. The rain had changed into balls of ice—HAIL!

This was typical opening weekend weather, something expected. Oh well—in a couple of weeks the sun will be out, insects will begin to hatch and fishing will be comfortable and forgotten will be the 27 degrees.

The Assassin

There are thousands and thousands of fly patterns. Every time someone ties a different fly, that person gets to name that pattern. I have named all of my original flies, e.g. "Special K," an attractor bucktail, "P²," a nymph imitation containing peacock herl and partridge and a "HEP," because it contained fur from a Hare's Ear and Hungarian Partridge hackle. Not very original but easy to remember.

Some flies are simply named in the honor of the originator: the Hendrickson, Edson Tiger, Gibbs Striper Fly and the Wulff series. Other flies are named for the material used to tie them: the Squirrel Tail, Pheasant Tail and the Hare's Ear nymph. Some flies for the bait it imitates: Red Ant, Mosquito, Black Midge, Black Gnat, Muddler Minnow and the Black Nosed Dace. Some time the name combines the material and the tyer's name, the Quill Gordon. Some time the material used and insect combined produce the Elk Hair Caddis.

Colors play an important role in the naming of flies. Black is commonly used, as well as other primary colors. More subtle colors are also used: Ginger Quill, Blue-Dun Spider, Brown Hackle, March Brown, Maple Syrup and the White, Gray, or Brown Wulff.

Flies are also named for the home waters it was used on or developed for: Parmachene Belle, Skykomish Sunrise and the Miller's River Special (originated by my mentor, Paul Kukkonen).

Some are named after the tyers profession: Royal Coachman, Lady Doctor, Supervisor, Colonel Bates and the Wardens Worry.

Then there are the whimsical names: Greenwell's Glory, Rat Faced MacDougal and Wickham's Fancy. Some sound like Heavy Metal Rock bands: Chartreuse Zonker, Stimulator, Wooly Bugger, Blue Angel or the Zoo Cougar.

Flies can change their names through the course of time. A Green Spot became the Nine-Three after the newly developed fly caught a nine pound three ounce salmon.

Another name change occurred when William Mills & Son sold a series of six bucktails of various colors, one of which was called the Red & Yellow Bucktail. John Alden Knight, of Pennsylvania, fished the red and yellow fly successfully for squaretails, and popularized it in his writings. He renamed the fly, calling it the Assassin. Weber Tackle Company began to sell the fly under yet another name. It went on to be one of the most popular flies ever tied. The Assassin was re-named for the knock-out-drops put in drinks, as seen in the film noir genre of motion pictures. The fly was supposed to knock fish out; it was called the Mickey Finn.

A Century Day

Lake Umbagog, pronounced (um-Bay-gog), straddles the Maine—New Hampshire border. The Indian word "Umbagog" means "shallow," and although it is a large lake, its average depth is only 14-feet. The land around Umbagog Lake has remained largely undeveloped and supports one of the largest nesting concentrations of loons, osprey and eagles.

In the olden days, Lake Umbagog was a cold water fishery containing brook and lake trout. In the late twentieth century it was illegally stocked with smallmouth bass. The bass thrived, much to the detriment of the native brook trout. The bass are now well established and moving into prime brook trout rivers, such as the Rapid River. Presently there is a huge effort to stop the spread of bass and protect the remaining wild brook trout population.

My fishing buddy, Bill, read an article in a bass fishing magazine about fishing in this gem of a lake. So at O-dark-thirty in the morning, we hooked up his bass-boat and headed north. We stopped for last minute supplies in Errol, and then headed out Rt. 26 toward the boat landing.

Bill said the author of the fishing article fished the big cove at the south end of the lake, so that's where we headed. After 3 hours, casting large heavy bass flies with our 8-weight rods, we had landed 6 small smallmouth bass, a little disappointing.

Always willing to explore, Bill said, "Let's get out of here, and try the north end." He started the engine and we sped north.

Bill pulled into a sheltered cove and switched over to the electric motor. Bill's first cast produced the 7th bass, and I shortly added number 8 to Bill's clicker. By the time we finished fishing the cove, the clicker registered 29 bass. "We could catch 50 fish today," Bill said, as we headed to the next cove. At 45 fish, I said, "If we reach 50, I'm going to switch to my 5-weight, my arm is getting tired." Bill agreed. Twenty minutes later we had caught the 50th smallmouth bass.

We had been fishing about 8 hours and we were tired and hungry. Bill reached into the cooler for sub-sandwiches and drinks that we had bought in Errol. Refreshed, we rigged up our lighter rods and headed for the next cove. 51, 52, 53, 54, 55, "At this rate we could reach 100," Bill joked. For a short stretch, every cast produced a hit. Around 6pm we were at the northernmost point in the lake. The clicker showed 89 fish. "One more cove, then we better head back, I don't want to be on an unfamiliar lake after dark," Bill said.

We had had a great day on the water and had seen many loons and osprey. In one of the coves an eagle sat in a tree just above our heads and launched himself into flight as we passed by.

Hot and pleasantly tired, we trailered the boat and headed home. Bill told me that this was the most fish he had ever caught in a single day. We caught 18 more bass on the way back to the landing, bringing the total for the day to 107—a century day.

Brown Leaves & Gray Skies

"All the leaves are brown, and the sky is gray"—this line is from the song "California Dreaming," popularized by The Mamas and the Papas, Jose Feliciano and The Manhattan Transfer. It is this kind of day that stirs the souls of fishermen everywhere. No thoughts of being "safe and warm if I was in LA." Cold windy fall days make me want to string up my long-rod, tie on a Woolly Bugger or Muddler Minnow or any large bushy streamer and hit the water. For it is days when the leaves are brown and the sky is gray, with cold blustery winds, that large trout feed aggressively, preparing for the short-days of winter.

Dreams of days past always seem to hold remembrances of catching lots and lots of fish. My oldest memory is of a teenager fishing Lake Quinsigamond one fall day. All the leaves were brown and the sky was gray, accompanied by heavy gusty cold winds. Not a pleasant day to be on an exposed shoreline.

I was just beginning to fish with flies, and had little previous experience; everything was new to me. All I knew about fly-fishing came out of books. I walked out on a gravel bar and began casting a Brass Hat streamer that I had tied myself. With the waves breaking at my feet, I was only able to cast 30 or 35 feet into the wind. I would cast as far as I could into the heavy chop and retrieve the fly in short jerks trying to make my fly imitate a wounded minnow. Suddenly, I felt a heavy pull on the end of my line and I was fast on to a fish. I caught several very respectable brown trout that day despite the strong wind and short casts. It was experiences like those that started me on the road to becoming a full-time fly fisherman.

Late last year, at the end of the trout season, I was fishing a pond in the Great North Woods. The leaves were brown and the sky was gray, not only gray but with hard rain falling. The air and water were cold but I was fairly comfortable enclosed in my fleece, waders and rain jacket.

I was casting an oversized Muddler Minnow searching for an oversized trout when I first noticed, what I thought, was a coconut floating on the water. I started to pay more attention to it when it began to move. I then noticed a second and third coconut. When the coconuts swam closer, I saw they were otters. Two additional otters joined these three. They frolicked in the water for a while then went ashore to run amuck among the cattails and bushes. A large log lay along the shore and the otters would creep up behind the log and pop their head over the top and watch me fish—five coconuts in a row. Five more reasons I keep fly-fishing.

As long as all the leaves are brown and the sky is gray, I will continue fishing these short, cold, windy days.

911

My Fishing Log for 9/11/2001 recorded the water temperature, air temperature, weather conditions, fish caught, flies used and the events that unfolded that day.

Angel and I had fished the eastern shore of the Androscoggin River, below the Errol dam. Early-afternoon we decided to move to the west shore. We hopped in the car and drove the short distance to the other side. As we got out of the car, a truck roared in behind us. The driver jumped out and gruffly started a conversation that went something like this:

Driver: What are you guys doing here?

Ray: We were fishing the other side and decided to try fishing on this side.

Driver: Do you know what's going on out there?

Angel: No, we have been fishing all morning and have no clue.

Driver: The Twin Towers in New York have been hit by terrorists and are burning.

Angel: Yeah—sure—and Rome is burning. I don't believe it; you're kidding us.

Ray: Angel, I believe it—how could he, and why would he, make up a story like that.

Driver: No, really, terrorists crashed two airplanes into the towers and they are burning.

Ray: We didn't have the radio on and had no idea of what's going on in the outside world.

Driver: Do you mind moving your car outside the gate? I am about to lock the gate—don't want the dam to get blown up.

As we moved the car, we put the radio on and everything the driver told us was confirmed. We learned that the Pentagon had also been hit and all flights had been grounded. We were also told that one of the flights was an American Airlines flight emanating from Boston. My brother-in-law is a pilot for American flying out of Boston. Angel, being from New York, called his sister who weepingly told him about her friends and family that were affected by the tragedy.

On the drive home we listened to the radio. In total amazement we were told the Twin Towers burned and collapsed. Lower Manhattan had been totally closed off. All the bridges were secured. Fire and rescuers from near and far were on the scene.

Angel and I reminisced about our connections to New York City. I was living in Brooklyn Heights at the time construction of the World Trade Center was nearing completion. I told him, I was consulting on the re-opening of the Brooklyn Navy Yard for Seatrain Shipyard. Seatrain (a shipping company) planned to design and build a fleet of VLCC's (Very Large Crude Carriers). My apartment was directly across the river with a view of the World Trade Center, and I watched the Towers construction every morning and evening.

People remember where they were and what they were doing the day JFK was shot. Everyone will also remember where he or she was and what they were doing the day the Twin Towers were destroyed. Angel and I will certainly always remember the Androscoggin River as the place we were and what we were doing on 911.

Assabet

After my discharge from the Navy, one of my first work assignments was mapping the SuAsCo Water Management Project. The Sudbury-Assabet-Concord watershed is located in the metro-west area of Boston, Massachusetts. It encompasses a large network of tributaries that flow into the Merrimack River. The Assabet River flows north about 30 miles from its headwaters in Westborough, through the centers of Northborough, Hudson, and Maynard, to its confluence with the Sudbury River where the Concord River begins.

After a four-year hiatus, I was just beginning to get back to fishing. In the process of scouting the SuAsCo watershed I found a section of the Assabet River resembling the famous chalk streams of England. Like the River Test and LeTort River, the Assabet's clear water flowed slowly through the open countryside. Like the River Test and the LeTort, the river was rich with aquatic vegetation, insect life and a population of one to 2-pound brown trout.

At my first opportunity, I returned to the river with rod in hand and walked down to the water's edge. I saw a couple of trout downstream rising for something. I walked along the bank to get within casting distance but when I got in position, the trout disappeared. I noticed a couple more trout working below me. Again when I got in position the trout were gone. It was then

I remembered some of the techniques of fishing spring creeks. A stealthy approach would be required.

Keeping a low profile, I approached the next pair of trout on my knees. I watched as the trout steadily rose to something I could not see. I cast my size 12 Light Cahill to the next riser. I watched as the trout ran for cover into the streaming vegetation. My fly floated untouched, it looked like nothing I could see on the river.

I clearly had some homework to do. I dug out a couple of my fishing books, tied some smaller flies and returned to the Assabet ready to do battle with one of these oversized brownies. Although I was able to get into casting position without spooking the fish, there was something about my fly and/or presentation that were not to the trout's satisfaction. This was getting frustrating. I now realized why chalk stream fishing for brown trout was considered the most challenging.

Again I returned home fishless, only now determined to figure out how to catch these fish. Again I sat down and tied a few size 20 and 22 flies that resembled the small insects I had seen. I stopped at Paul's Fly Shop on Green Street and bought some 6X and 7X tippet material.

Returning to the river for the third time I rigged up my rod with a 15-foot leader tapered to a 7X tippet (.004" dia. with a breaking strength of .8 lb.) and tied on a black size 22 midge. I positioned myself to cast to one of the rising trout. I dropped the fly six feet up-stream of a two-pound brown trout that was actively feeding. I strained my eyes to watch the tiny fly slowly drift down to the fish and simultaneously watched the fish finning in the current. As the fly came into the trout's view, the large brown trout slowly rose to the surface and sucked in my fly, success at last.

I was beginning to understand this sport of fly-fishing.

L. L. Bean

One day as I was coming off the Mad River, I heard someone shouting "Ray!—Ray!—I have something for you." Howard Grimmes, of Waterville Valley, was doing the shouting. He had come across a book titled *Hunting-Fishing and Camping*," written by none other than L. L. Bean himself, and wanted to share it with me.

The inside cover had the price ($1.00) and the year it was Copyrighted (1944). This was about the time that my father started taking me fishing. My parents would take me to a small, nearby, city pond to fish for sunfish and perch. They told me that I would fill a bucket with water and put any fish I caught in the bucket. At the end of the day, I would count them and then dump them back in the pond.

I skimmed through the Hunting section of LL's book and skipped over some grizzly pictures of dead animals that were either shot or trapped. I did get a kick out of a list of wearing apparel for hunters: "Shoes—Leather Top Rubbers, Stockings—knee-length heavy woolen and two pair of light woolen. Pants—One pair medium weight all wool with zipper bottom. Coat—One medium weight, all wool, red and black with game pocket in back." I remembered owning all these clothes and that they weighed a ton.

The Camping section covered many topics. "How to Choose a Tent, How to Build a Bough Bed, Grub Lists and other Camping Hints." The Camping section, like most of the rest of the book, contained obsolete information. Today's modern equipment and made-made materials completely replaced equipment and techniques discussed in the book.

The Fishing section had chapters titled; "How to Fish for Salmon, Trout and Togue, How to Care for Minnows and Worms, How to Fish for Small Brook Trout" and four chapters on Fly Fishing. These chapters contained a lot of ancient history. There was a chart to fit rods, (Medium Action and Stiff Action) to lines. Lines were measured by diameter. "A," thinnest to "G," the thickest. Snelled Parmacheene Belle, Montreal, Silver Doctor, Red Ibis, Black Gnat and Royal Coachman wet flies were illustrated. Split bamboo rods were being replaced with fiberglass rods. All equipment I started fishing with.

A picture of a Mr. Bean holding a couple of large land-locked salmon as well as several other old photographs appear in the book. Those were the days of keeping limit catches. Most of the fish were caught on a "Live Bait Fly". This lure was made by sewing a minnow on a streamer fly. A lure I am not familiar with.

Although most of the information was dated, this book certainly brought back many memories. I am sure any angler with a little gray hair would enjoy browsing through L. L. Bean's book.

Fishing Feathers

I enjoy watching trout rise to the feathers on my flies. Sometime I get to see the opposite—feathers (birds) fishing for fish. I once had a loon dive under the canoe that I was fishing from and take a brook trout off my hook. Eagles, the top of the avian food chain, are making a strong come back. I have seen them searching for unwary fish over Lake Umbagog and Squam Lake.

Ospreys are fascinating to watch as they soar over lakes searching for prey. I remember watching an osprey survey a large water hazard at a PGA golf tournament in Hartford, Connecticut. The pond was surround by three signature holes, the 15th, 16th and 17th. Even though it was the 4th and final round of play, many people watched the osprey fold its wings, dive into the water and fly away with a fish in its talons.

I especially like to watch kingfishers. Kingfishers, for those not familiar with them, look like large blue jays with oversized heads. They sit near the top of an overhanging tree and wait for a fish to swim by. When the bird spots a fish, it gently pushes off, and with wings folded, dives into the water. Their action always reminds me of the old Tarzan movies, when Tarzan dives off a cliff. The kingfisher hits the water with a loud splash and nails the target. When they are feeding on fish, it sounds as if someone is throwing big rocks into the water.

Great Blue Herons are another of my favorite birds too watch. One warm spring day, I was standing in the middle of the

Androscoggin River fishing for trout and salmon when I noticed a Great Blue Heron behind me. He was standing about a foot from shore, in a riffle under a tree, in ankle deep water (his ankle). The riffle appeared about two inches deep, a place I would never cast my fly. I watched the bird patiently standing there, all the while thinking that the bird had not selected a very likely fishing spot and would most likely go hungry that day. Suddenly the Heron's head darted forward into the river and came out with a pound of brook trout. The fish was so large the bird's head bobbed up and down as the flopping trout tried to escape. I was given a fishing lesson that day.

I cringe every time I see a bird take a trout, feeling as if they are depriving me of my recreation, but then I remind myself that I am using their feathers to lure trout.

Dew Drop Inn

The cream-colored mayfly imitation contrasted with the dark water and sky as it gently floated downstream. The fly began making ripples on the surface of the water indicating the fly line was dragging and it was time for another cast.

I was standing along the edge of Hewitt Pond, a large pool in a river formed by a small dam, located in southeastern Connecticut. The pond was named for Edward R. Hewitt, who had a great influence on nymph fishing in the USA. Today he is perhaps best known for his three stages of a fly-fisherman's development: (1) catch as many fish as possible, (2) catch a large fish, (3) to catch as difficult a fish as possible. I would add a 4th and final stage, (4) fishing for the pure enjoyment of fishing. Hewitt also advanced the view that the presentation of the fly was extremely important: the main thing, according to him, was not to have as great a range of flies as possible, but to have a smaller quantity and be able to present them correctly.

Trout were steadily rising for hatching mayflies. There were several varieties of mayflies on the water that evening. Dark brown March Browns, along with light gray Hendricksons, floated slowly in the current. The predominant insect was clearly the Light Cahill that I was imitating.

Behind me was a dense forest, prohibiting any sort of back cast. Roll casting was the only option. I stripped in the slack and gently raised my rod tip. With a quick snap I brought the rod tip down; the line formed a circle that rolled out until the line was straight. The Light Cahill fell quietly on the water and began another float.

I continued roll casting, watching the fly drift with the flow of the river and the trout rise to mayflies a foot away from my imitation. A few trout actually had the nerve to jump over my line in order to get to one of the real mayflies. These antics accentuated the difficulties of catching trout in a slow moving stream where they have every opportunity to examine the fly.

Swallows skimmed the surface picking off mayflies at will. They left dimples behind similar to the dimples of the trout sucking in the insects. I changed to a much smaller Light Cahill and roll cast it out. As soon as it hit the water a wild brook trout smashed it.

I wish I could say, I found the secret of the day, but it was the only fish I caught. It was just a fluke that the fish hit after I changed flies.

At dark, I reeled in my fly, and walked back to my car. I was content that I didn't get shut out, and would return to the wild brookies rising to a mayfly hatch. I drove a short distance to the Dew Drop Inn and had the meatloaf special, and slept the sleep of a happy man.

Clean Sweep

April! The rivers were running and the ice was off the pond. It was time to prepare for, and go on the first fishing trip of the year—a shake-down cruise, so to speak.

I prepared by checking my fly boxes and replenishing my favorite flies. I stripped all the fly lines off the reels and straightened, cleaned and lubricate them; leaders and tippets were repaired or replaced and my fishing vest was reloaded. I dug out my long underwear, fleece pants, triple thick shirt and rain jacket. I have not forgotten how cold it got sitting in 38° water.

I lowered float tube from the garage rafters and assembled the pump, kick fins, landing net, boots and waders.

As I drove to the pond, I become a little apprehensive. My float tube was several years old and my waders were new and not yet christened. I slipped on my waders and inflated the float tube; giving it a few extra pumps to compensate for the contraction it was going to see when it hit the cold water.

I walked to the water edge. The water was blue and the sky was bluer. I slid the float tube into the water, backed into it and gently sat down, secure in my little world. Because I had a mixture of old and new equipment, I decided to stay close to shore for a while.

Convinced all my gear was functioning properly, I started kicking for the north shore. Bill once told me that the north end of lakes always warm up first in the spring and I have yet to prove him wrong.

The north end of the pond was shallow with dark brown leaves covering the bottom, perfect for the sun's rays to do its thing. To make it even better, the cove contained Large Woody Debris (a few fallen trees). I fished up and down the cove a couple of times, casting onto the shallow shelf and slowly retrieving the soft hackle fly. I saw the bottom clearly but did not see any cruising fish.

On my third pass through the cove I felt a slight resistance to my fly. I gently raised my rod tip and was fast to a fish. The fish was in about a foot of water. I could see the trout was of respectable size, easily the largest first fish of any previous season. The fish rushed toward deeper water. As I worked the fish closer, I could see it was a brown trout, golden with red and black spots on the sides. I slid the net under him and lifted him onto my casting apron. The trout's sides glowed gold in the late afternoon sun as I slipped the barbless hook out of his lip; with one last admiring glance, I gently slipped him back into the water where he belonged.

All my gear functioned as designed. A U S Navy ship returning from a successful shake-down cruise secures a broom to the highest mast. My first fishing trip was indeed—a clean sweep.

Orange²

It's always an adventure trying new waters, never knowing what you're going to find. Recently, Angel and I decided to drive west, and fish two ponds that were near each other, Tewksbury Pond in Grafton, and Orange Pond in Orange.

We decided to fish Tewksbury first because at 46-acres it was the larger of the two ponds. Maps indicated a public landing at the south end of the pond and road proximity at the north end. The south end was the deep end. We decided to fish the north end as the depth maps showed some nice flats that the trout might be cruising in search of insect life.

After parking in a pull-off by the side of the road we carried our gear and float tubes a 1/8 mile or so along an abandoned railroad bed and descended a steep bank to the water's edge. On walking to a spot where we could launch our tubes, I saw a couple of risers. Angel kicked to the area and quickly caught a brookie. We fished for a couple more hours, during which Angel got a couple more brookies and a brown trout.

Our next pond was Orange Pond, a smaller pond of 28-acres and shallower with an average depth of 8-feet. We drove along the dirt road looking for the pond but realized we passed it after seeing the end of the pond through a field. We turned around, checked our map, and promptly found the launch area. With the tubes re-inflated, we began fishing. I decided to kick across the pond and fish the far shore. Angel said he was going to fish a channel in the center of the pond.

When I got to the far shore, I could see some surface action at the far northwest end of the pond. The cove was the lee shore so I kicked west. The risers looked like tiny fish, small perch or dace maybe, but what did I have to lose. As I got closer I could see that they were trout sipping midges. I quickly re-rigged for top water fishing. When I got within casting range of a rising trout, I dropped my fly three feet to the left of the next rise. Wham! I was fast to a nice brookie.

Angel fished his way to the west end of the pond, picking up a few brookies and a couple of small rainbow trout along the way. We watched the trout rise off the bottom and take our dry flies. Most casts were aimed at a riser and answered with a hit. The surface action continued non-stop for the rest of the afternoon. Orange Pond in Orange, New Hampshire, provided, that day at least, brook trout fishing at its best.

Monster of Kettle Creek

June found Angel and me back in Pennsylvania, fishing the spring creeks. Our host, Rocco Rosamilia, suggested we hit Kettle Creek for the evening hatch. He told us a couple of monster trout, estimated to be 7 and 9-pounds, had been seen cruising the river. He went on to say the river was warmer this year resulting in a slower catch rate.

We arrived at Kettle Creek and scanned the water for any activity. No fish were showing. We were not surprised as it was only late afternoon and we did not expect the hatches to begin until later that evening. We continued to watch the river as we ate our dinner. Dinner consisted of a delicious (food always tastes better outdoors) tuna grinder washed down by a bottle of ice-tea.

Angel and I suited up and waded into the river. Rocco put his hand in the water and called out to tell us the water temperature was high, in the high 60s. I dropped my stream thermometer into the creek, it registered 76°. Rocco said my thermometer must be broken because the creek's temperature had never been that high. When Angel's stream thermometer verified the 76° reading, Rocco responded that it was unusual to have two broken thermometers.

After a fishless half-hour, Rocco told us to reel up and we would go searching for cooler water. As we drove upstream, Rocco said he thought Hammersley Fork area might be cooler. Upon arriving, Angel and I waded down the Hammersley Creek to the junction with Kettle Creek. Two thermometers dropped into the water, 69°, a little better. Almost immediately trout began to rise. Rocco cautioned us to be vigilant as those monster trout had most likely moved up to these cooler waters.

Shortly a nice brookie rose to my #16 Royal Trude fished on a 6X tippet. Angel was also fastened to a nice brook trout. Obviously Rocco made the right call. On my next cast, a giant rainbow rose and sucked in my Royal Trude. As the fish turned and flashed its wide red-striped side, my jaw dropped. This was one of the monsters Rocco had been talking about. I wish I could report landing the monster and show folks a grip-and-grin picture of me with the monster trout but simply put, the 6X tippet was not strong enough to hold the fish. The 6X leader parted on the rainbow's first run. I was not super-disappointed; I would have released the fish and because I will always have a mental picture of that monster rainbow rising to my fly.

Angel and I continued to catch brookies, rainbows and a few browns until it got so dark we couldn't see anymore. On the drive back, Rocco talked about the two broken thermometers and Angel and I talked about the fish we caught.

Even though the conditions were less than ideal, Angel and I caught our share of fish and found the monster of Kettle Creek.

Ellis River

The orange Humpy floated over the rainbow trout as he slowly maneuvered to maintain his position in the river. The Humpy had floated unmolested over the fish a dozen times. Time to change flies. I tried other dry flies, the Usual, Adams and Cooper Bug, all with similar results. Actually there were two rainbows that I could see in the same slow run of the river.

I was fishing below the covered bridge on the Ellis River in Jackson, New Hampshire. The river has a grand beginning; it drains the eastern side of Mount Washington. Nelson Brook draining Huntington Ravine, Cutler River draining Tuckerman Ravine and New River draining the Gulf of Slides join to form the Ellis River, which then flows south paralleling Rt. 16, through Jackson, emptying into the Saco River below Glen.

The New Hampshire fishing regulations contain special rules for the Ellis River. From the covered bridge in Jackson to the Iron Railroad Bridge in Glen, it is fly-fishing only, with a daily limit of 2 brook trout. The remainder of the river is open to the general fishing regulations; 5 fish or 5-pounds, whichever comes first.

I had been tossing dry flies at these two fish for close to an hour. It was time to try some nymphs. A March Brown Spider, Gold-ribbed Hare's Ear, Prince and Pheasant Tail nymphs all passed unmolested. I was encouraged by the fact that each time I changed flies the trout would swim up to the flies and give them a close inspection before rejecting them.

I concluded that they would hit the right fly with the right presentation. Time to try some streamers. The Mickey Finn, Black Zonker, Black Nosed Dace and White Marabou streamers had the same result as the nymph.

Normally I would have moved on long ago but it is hard to leave fish to find fish, especially when they continued to show some interest. During this last session I noticed a third rainbow darting back and forth about thirty feet below the two I was fishing over. I adjusted my casting position to give the new guy a try. Same result.

Moving back to the first two trout, I re-tied the orange Humpy. On the first cast, one of the rainbows shot up and smashed the fly. I managed to hook and lose the second trout a short time later. After a thousand casts, showing them my best flies, the trout decided to hit the fly I started with. How to explain it?

Bass Bugging

The canoe was on the car roof, the drinks and sandwiches were in the cooler. Larry and I were headed toward a local pond to do some late evening and nighttime bugging for largemouth bass.

We positioned ourselves between two patches of lily pads and proceeded to work the edges. We would cast our bass bugs to the pads, let them lie still for as long as we could stand it, then gave them a twitch. The cork body flies were supposed to imitate frogs, mice, birds or any large thing that happened to fall into the water.

Larry suggested we eat our sandwich before it got too dark to see. He cast his fly to the middle of the open water and set his rod across his lap. He unwrapped an Italian club sandwich and poured himself a glass of Chianti. As he ate his sandwich the bass bug drifted motionless. As Larry took a bite, an enormous largemouth bass rocketed out of the water like a submarine launched Polaris missile, turned in midair, with his mouth wide open, dove straight down on the frog colored lure. Larry's hands were hopelessly compromised, so he tried to set the hook with his lap. To this day I tell the story about the bass, and play the 3D-IMAX film in my mind of this huge bass in mid-air, with Larry, balancing a glass of Chianti and a submarine sandwich, jerking his knees trying to set the hook.

As night fell we cast blindly to a target outlined against the sky; listen for the sound of the bass bug hitting the water then retrieve the fly with a very slow twitching action. I could judge distance by feeling the weight of the line beyond the rod tip, and for the most part, land my fly on target. Occasionally the water would explode and we would set the hook.

On one of my casts, I worked out about thirty or forty feet of line and with a single-haul shot the air-resistant fly forward. I waited for the plopping sound signaling a safe landing for the bass bug. No plop. I waited for what seemed like a long time, when suddenly my line started to rise. I could feel twitching at the end of my rising line but could see nothing. I told Larry what was happening and asked him to stand by.

I slowly pulled in the line straining to see into the darkness. Whatever was on the end of my line did not live in water. The end of the line continued to flutter. Finally I could see the end of my off-white fly line and the beginning of my leader. I reached for the leader and slowly pulled it in. We shined a flashlight on the end of my leader and saw a bat. The leader had wrapped itself around the bat's wing. I carefully reached around the bat and cut my fly off, allowing the leader to slip free. The bat and I were glad to see each other go our own separate ways.

Shortly after midnight we slowly paddled our way back to the boat landing being very careful not to hit any submerged objects in the dark. We did not keep any of the bass we caught that night. We did however keep a wonderful mental vision of a lassoed bat and that huge bass in mid-air.

The Fish That Got Away

Boy Scouts must know how to tie the Square Knot, Sheet Bend, and Clove Hitch to succeed. Boating sailors can tie a Bowline, Anchor Hitch and Cleat Hitch in order to secure their boats. A Navy sailor can splice a line, tie a Monkeys Fist, Turk's Head, Wall and Crown and a Chain Sinnet. I was all three.

Knots are also critical to fly-fishermen. My uncle, Henry (a Signalman in the Navy), taught me to tie knots. This knowledge served me well as a Boy Scout and Sailor. Although I never had a reason to tie, other than to demonstrate, a Sheep Shank (used to shorten a line); I still remember how to tie it.

A good knot should be easy to tie, have high knot efficiency (breaking strength), not slip under strain, and not jam (easily un-tied). *The Ashley Book of Knots*, (Clifford W. Ashley), has been my reference book for years. It explains "every practical knot, what it looks like, who uses it, where it comes from, and how to tie it."

Fishermen, like sailors, depend on their knots to hold fast. They must be proficient in tying knots, and must be able to tie them in the dark, in the cold, and tie them with thin, hair-like, 7x (.004" dia.) leaders.

Fly-fishing gear consists of several components that are connected with knots. The backing is attached to the reel with an Arbor Knot. The backing can be connected to the fly line with a Nail Knot or a loop-to-loop connection. The neatest loop knot is the Perfection Loop, my choice. Easier to tie is the Surgeons Loop. The leader, a tapered monofilament line separating the thick fly line and the fly, may use the same two knots.

The tippet, a thin section of monofilament extending the leader, is usually tied to the leader with a Blood Knot or Surgeons Knot. I use the Blood Knot because of its symmetry. The final, and probably the most important connection, is the tippet to the fly. My preference is the Improved Clinch Knot. The Turle Knot can be used with heavier lines, 3x (.008") and up.

There are many other knots that can be used, but the above knots will serve well in most conditions. One other knot fly-casters' are familiar with, is the Wind Knot. During casting, the line may form a loop and the end passes through the loop forming a knot. The wind gets the blame for this, but I blame the fisherman and call it, the Casting Knot.

It is imperative that repairs to frayed leaders and compromised knots be repaired immediately. This is inevitably when a big fish will hit, and provide stories of the fish that got away.

Head for the Hills

August! And the air is HOT. We head for cooler places. The snowbirds migrate from the southern states and city folk's rush to the seaside or mountains. The water gets warm and trout head for their summer haunts. In lakes or ponds the coldwater species swim to a depth where the temperature and saturated oxygen is to their satisfaction. In streams and rivers they move upstream to cooler headwaters or downstream to deep water.

The White Mountain Area and The Great North Woods both have many rivers and streams that remain fishable all summer. Tributaries tend to run cooler than the larger rivers. The headwaters of these tributaries are most likely the coolest with some mountain streams remaining in the 50° and 60° range. On an 80° August day the water in these tributary brooks can feel downright frigid. Rivers that run through forests tend to remain cooler that rivers on valley floors. My fishing-log indicates a temperature increase of 1° for every 1 to 3 miles for forested rivers. Rivers that flow through open valley floors may have a temperature increase of 3° to 6° for every mile.

I head for the hills in August. I carry two very small fly boxes in my pocket, one for dry flies and one for wet flies and streamers. The wild brook trout remain active in the cooler tributaries. They are not very selective, as there are not many hatches in these rocky, acidic waters. They will aggressively hit most all of the popular dry and wet fly patterns along with grasshopper, beetle, ant or other terrestrial imitations.

I carry clippers, forceps, floatant, thermometer and tippet material on a neck lanyard, leaving the heavy vest at home. I use a 6½-foot, 2-weight rod that I made especially for use on smaller rivers and its tributaries. I wear hip boots with felt soles for a better grip on the slippery rocks, but I could easily wet-wade.

August is the time to break out the topo maps and look for the rivers and brooks in higher elevations. Look for rivers and tributaries that drain the higher peaks of the White Mountains and run through shaded forests. There are many hiking trails that parallel brooks. It's amazing how some of these tiny water flows can hold some nice wild brook trout. Armed with the above information it is time to head for the hills.

Quilt Show

The kayak eased slowly over the shallow stone-covered bar. I paddled to port avoiding a large rock that rose to within an inch of the surface. Looking ahead, watching for more rocks, I noticed what looked like, a 3-pound smallmouth bass moving toward deeper water. I was on Great Pond, one of the seven Belgrade Lakes in Maine, scouting fishing sites.

Great Pond inspired Ernest Thomson's to write the play, *On Golden Pond*, home to, "Walter," the humongous trout Norman and Billy caught and released in Purgatory Cove.

The annual Maine Quilt show was about to start. My wife, Pat, and her friend Nancy, owner of the former Calico Cupboard quilt shop, were taking a quilt design class. Joe, Nancy's husband, was playing golf with our host, Paul. Our hostess, Louise, was busy getting ready for the quilt show. Louise and Paul, owners of Great Pond Quilts, were vendors at the show and were displaying their pre-cut quilt kits. Louise and Paul own a summer camp on Great Pond, and graciously invited us to stay at their camp.

The seven lakes in the Belgrade chain are North Pond, East Pond, Salmon and McGrath Ponds, Long Pond, Great Pond and finally Messalonskee Lake. All seven lakes are part of the Messalonskee Stream drainage, which is one of the tributaries to the Kennebec River. Years ago the lakes were well known for great catches of salmon and brook trout, with regular reports of large salmon and brook trout. Today, there are few salmon because of the diminished smelt population. In the mid-twentieth century smallmouth bass were introduced and thrived in their new home pushing out the brook trout.

I first heard of the Belgrade Lakes many years ago. At that time it had a great reputation for smallmouth bass. Today the biggest draw to the Belgrade lakes is northern pike. The pike were illegally stocked and like the smallmouth thrived in their new home. Each time new species was introduced, it pushed out other fish.

The next morning, I mounted my kayak and headed back to the stony-point with the cruising smallmouth. I cast a large bass-size Special K, on my floating line for forty minutes before I got my first fish, a 1-pound smally. That kept me on the shallow flats for another forty minutes. With no additional hits, I decided, if I were a smallmouth I would move to deeper-cooler water. I changed to my ten-foot sink tip line and tied on a chartreuse Clouser (it's got no use, if it's not chartreuse). I moved to where the bottom dropped away. After fishing the drop-off for a short time, I got a vicious strike. The fish jumped three times and then dove for the bottom. The bass towed the kayak around for a while; finally it came to the surface. I lipped the 3-pound smallmouth, removed the hook, released the fish and watched the bass slowly swim away.

Time to go see some quilts; after all, I was the fishing the Belgrade Lakes because of the Quilt Show.

Pencil Sketch

As I approached the pond I could see a woman sitting in a chair with a sketchpad in her lap. I recognized the woman as I got closer. Maryellen is a painter and printmaker who makes Waterville Valley her second home. She has over thirty years of teaching art to both adults and children. She leads the White Mountain Painters, a group of local artists working on site outdoors in the Waterville Valley area. With permission, I looked over her shoulder and saw the pencil drawing of the pond that she was working on; it included her husband David, who was wading the shoreline casting a fly. As if on cue, he caught and landed a brook trout.

David told me he ordered and a received a float tube and would like to try it out and asked if I would accompany him on his first float tube fishing trip and provide some guidance. I told him I would be glad to, and we made arrangements to meet three days later.

As I drove up to meet him, I found him on his front lawn assembling his new bright-blue Fish Cat 4 float tube. "It was a tight fit getting the foam in the seat and back," he said. I acknowledged that fact and reminded him that you only have to do it once. He commented on my silver-gray Fishcat and was surprised when I told him it also was a bright-blue when it was new but faded to this mellow color over the years. We packed his gear and were on our way.

After parking the car, we inflated the tubes, assembled our fly rods and put on our waders. It was a beautiful summer day with a strong sun shining. We put on our flippers at the water's edge. I advised walking backward with flippers on to avoid tripping. I walked into knee-deep water and positioned my float tube behind me and gently sat down. David followed suit and, being a swimmer, had no trouble manipulating his watercraft.

He tied on a caddis imitation, intending to fish the surface. I tied on a damselfly nymph, and planned to fish it just under the surface. The water registered in the low seventies on my thermometer, and the sun was bright. There were not many fish rising but enough to make it interesting. I kicked east and my fishing partner worked westward.

We worked around the entire pond getting a few responses from the resident brookies. Not as fast action as the previous week, but, oh well, it was nice to just be on the water on warm summer day with the new Fish Cat 4 working well. As I watched my fishing partner make his final cast, it reminded me of the sketch of an angler's fly line floating in the air above the water as shown in Maryellen's pencil sketch.

If I were a Pike

"If I were a pike, this is where I'd live," I said to Charlie. We had been fishing for brook trout on Lac Mabile, Labrador, and were about to break for lunch. As we beached our boat, I surveyed the patch of lily pads that ran parallel to shore. The lily pads ran for a couple hundred yards along the shore and were twenty to thirty yards wide. This was the largest area of aquatic growth we found on the lake.

On Charlie's first cast he was into a three foot long pike. I grabbed my 8-weight fly rod and walked along the shore checking out the pads. The 8-weight rod was designed to cast larger flies and handle larger fish. It was stiffer and stronger than my lighter 3 and 5-weight trout rods. I could see pike lying among the lily pads sunning themselves in the mid-day sun. The large pike look like logs. At one point it looked like an abandoned lumberyard.

I found a break in the pads and waded in. I cast my oversized white Zonker (rabbit-skin strip) near one of the logs. It turned quickly and moved toward my fly. I gave the fly a twitch and the log turned into a torpedo. The fish opened its jaws and engulfed the fly. As soon as I set the hook, the pike headed toward the weeds. If a pickerel in New Hampshire got tangled in the weeds, it would usually be lost. I could not stop or turn the pike to avoid the lily pads. But to my surprise the pike just swam through the weeds like they weren't there. The pike was so strong, my leader cut through the pad stems like a buzz saw. Minutes later I beached a 39-inch long pike; my first northern pike.

Charlie and I continued fishing the patch of lily pads for a couple more hours, hooking and landing the pike that lingered among the weeds. We finally broke for lunch, a couple of foot long brook trout that we saved for just this purpose. The inside meat was the deep red of a completely wild brook trout. In fact the Canadians call them "reds."

Later we fished the eskers (a narrow break in a glacial ridge connecting two lakes). Charlie on one side and me on the other. I caught my first whitefish, a couple more pike and a large red. I heard Charlie whooping and hollering on the other side of the break. I watched as he dipped the landing net into the water and lifted out a 44-inch long trophy pike.

Crystal Ball

"I would like to find a crystal ball," Angel said as we drove north for another Great North Woods, October, fishing trip. As we drove, we wondered if the fishing would be as good as in previous years. Having explored most of the waters in and around Colebrook, we did not expect to explore new waters, but would return to some of our favorites.

We would need a Crystal Ball to help decide which body of water to fish. We could stop at Mirror Lake, in Whitefield, or Christine Lake or South Pond, in Stark. These ponds had been good to us in the past. Fish Pond, Clarksville Pond, and Little Diamond Pond had all produced some nice fish. A few remote hike-in ponds held some potential. Rivers and streams in and around Colebrook include the Connecticut River, Mohawk River, Ammonoosuc River, Nash Stream plus a number of smaller brooks—all home to a population of coldwater fish.

We decided to stop at Christine Lake on the way up. I think it is one on the prettiest lakes in New Hampshire. Gin-clear water, surrounded by high hills and only a few camps on the far shore, allows one to enjoy a wilderness-like experience. For several years we unsuccessfully chased the elusive brown trout that were known to inhabit the lake. Maybe this year would be different. As we launched our float tubes, the resident loons welcomed us, or maybe they were telling us to leave their fish alone. We again remained troutless, but did manage to catch some smallmouth bass.

The rest of the trip was spent chasing native brook trout. We hopped from pond to pond and caught fish in all of them. The male brook trout were in full spawning colors—light blue and yellow spots against the dark olive body, and orange and white underside set off by striking white, black and orange fins. I think the brook trout is the prettiest of all the trout and char families.

On our last day of our annual October fishing trip in the Great North Woods, Angel and I were having our usual breakfast at Howard's Restaurant on Main Street in downtown Colebrook. Howard's is a popular eating establishment for politicians and presidential candidates because of its proximity to Dixville Notch, first town to count votes. The owner told us about some of the political candidates that stopped by during her 12 years of ownership. I asked if the politicians gave her advanced notice of arriving, and if she ever refused them from coming. She told me, they usually requested permission and indeed she had refused a few candidates.

Over bacon and eggs, Angel and I discussed our destination for the day. Should we head north or start south toward home? We reviewed the ponds that were on the way home without reaching any decision. The owner came along with more coffee, we explained our dilemma and asked for any guidance that she could provide. Her name was Crystal Ball.

Fishing with Izaak

I approached my beat on the River Test only to find someone fishing my assigned pool. "Good morning," I said, "I believe you are fishing my beat." "What's a beat?" he asked, "My name is Izaak Walton and I have fished here since 1633 without any problem." As we talked, it wasn't long before Izaak was reminiscing about the good old days.

He went on to tell me that when he started fishing, the line was simply tied to the end of a 12 to 14-foot pole; there were no reels. The line was made of horsehair. The first link (section) was made up of two to four pieces of hair from a horse's tail. Additional hairs were added to the following links until the desired length was reached. He went on to tell me that the hair from a white horse was the strongest. The links were attached with a water knot. I told him I had never heard of that knot. Isaak told me that he would show me how to tie it, but over the years had forgotten how to tie it now that he was using a store-bought tapered leader. He was sure it was in his book, *The Compleat Angler.*

The fly was swung out over the water and fished using three methods. The most popular was dapping. Holding the fly just above the water allowing the fly to skip over the water, imitating a mayfly laying its eggs. The second method was floating the fly on the surface simulating a mayfly dun or spinner and the third method was allowing the fly to sink, imitating an emerging nymph.

He went on to tell me some of his favorite flies. The Dun Stone, and older variations of the March Brown, Black Gnat, Cowdung and, a fly that was later "discovered" in the Ozark Mountains, the Wooly Worm—they overfilled his wooden fly box.

Hooks, in his time, were made from needles and had no eyes. The flies were snelled, that is, the horsehair was tied directly to the hook-shank.

Large trout were common in the old days. He admitted to throwing his rod in the river when he couldn't play a large fish, tactics that allowed him to land a trout nearly one yard long, whose outline was traced and hung in Rickabie's place in Ware.

Mr. Walton continued to cast his fly and as I watched, a huge brown trout rose and engulfed his fly. The trout must have been a yard long and easily weighed 20-pounds or more. The trout made a very loud disturbance that could be heard a long distance. After a short time, I realize the disturbance I was hearing was that of my alarm clock ringing.

The Usual

Bill: [Fly rod bent] I got one
Angel: [Quizzically] What fly are you using?
Bill: The Usual
     [A short time later]
Bill: I got another one.
Angel: [Annoyingly] What fly are you using?
Bill: The Usual
Angel: [Quietly to Ray] Why won't Bill tell me the name of the fly?
Ray: He is telling you what he is using; the name of the fly is "The Usual."

One dismal afternoon, Fran Betters was in his Adirondack Sport Shop on the New York's West Branch of the Ausable River tying up a batch of Haystacks (a dry fly with a deer hair tail and upright wing). He noticed a snowshoe hare's foot lying on the top on his tying bench and he decided to substitute the wiry pad-hairs and under-fur for the Haystacks deer hair. This experimental fly was actually tested by a friend of Fran's. The Ausable trout readily accepted the fly and the fly soon became a local favorite. Whenever he was asked what fly had hooked a large trout, he would answer, somewhat annoyingly "The Usual."

Although the Haystack is still around, I believe The Usual is a much better fly. I believe Mr. Betters, many years ago, recognized the characteristics of a snowshoe hare's foot would be an improvement. The long fibers of the snowshoe hare's foot are translucent and flexible giving the fly a lifelike movement; also the hare's hair repels water. My favorite attribute is its floatability; the fly can be dried with a couple of false-casts. I personally prefer flies with a vague, impressionistic, outline rather than an exact imitation of one particular insect.

Several years later I was fishing with my friend David and caught several brookies on The Usual and relayed the story of Angel and Bill's conversation about the fly. Three days later I received this note;

"Ray: I was looking through my fly box and found a collection of flies that you donated to the WVAIA which I bid on and won. Much to my surprise, it included, 'The Usual.' There was a small hatch going on in the lee of the wind, near the rock island, so I tied on 'The Usual,' and instantly it was inhaled by a brookie! I continued to catch fish, until the fly was too soggy to fluff up. The ability of 'The Usual' to catch fish is the most dramatic example of catching fish by not matching the hatch. How can such an ugly, puff-of-fuzz catch so many fish? Please, please show me how to tie it."

Signed

David

Walter with Shad

L to R—Allen, Bill & Jack

Angel at Willard Pond

Bill with 100th Small.mouth Bass

Ray with Gray Jay

Tailwater Terror—Bill & Jack

Angel in Chalk Stream   Charlie with Trophy Pike

Tim Pond L to R—
Bill, Jack, Angel & Ray

Angel in Fish Cat 4

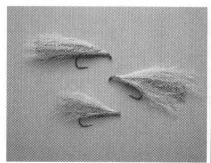

Mickey Finns

The Usual

Leather Tails & the Falcon

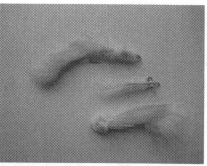

Trigger Flies; Chartreuse Zonker,
Clouser, Zoo Cougar

Holiday Hex

Special K

Ray & Rocco with LWD (Large Woody Debris)

Ray—Grip & Grin with Brook Trout

Tiger Trout   Brown Trout

Spider-Man

My fly box is full of spiders. Not the eight-legged kind of spiders, but the soft hackle style of wet flies. Wet flies are tied with wings; spiders (aka, soft hackles) are wingless.

This style of fly was originated in England and has been around for hundreds of years. A little research of these spiders indicated that James E. Leisenring recognized that trout like to feed on insects that are in the transition stage from nymph form to adult form, sometimes called emergers. These insect forms do not have wings, leading to the idea of a wet fly without wings, but with legs fully apparent. Legs made of soft hackle move in a natural, enticing way. Hackle, are the soft feathers from a bird's neck or saddle. When wrapped around a hook imitate legs.

My fly box previously held modern realistic imitations of nymphs, Copper Johns, Peasant Tails, and Fox nymphs. Several years ago I tied on a Breadcrust, simple body and two turns of grizzly hackle, as a dropper behind my dry fly. At the end of the day, I realized that I had caught most of the fish on the dropper. Over the following years these soft hackles have pushed the modern nymphs out of my fly box because of their effectiveness and their ease of tying.

I tie my spiders with three body colors, black, tan and olive. I have used dubbing, floss, and wool for body material. The color and type of material used for the bodies has not, over the years, made a large difference in their fish-catching ability. If I had to choose one body material it would definitely be peacock hurl. The hackle, on the other hand, seems to be the key to success. The Hungarian partridge out-performs all the other hackles. Hen (chicken) hackle can be substituted. Starling hackle works well on the smaller size hooks because of its diminutive size.

There are many specific patterns that belong to the soft-hackle family. The oldest are flies like the Partridge and Green or Partridge and Orange, with other colors used to imitate different species of insects. The fly names refer simply to hackle (partridge) and to the color of the body. These kinds of flies are, thought by some, to imitate caddis emergers but others report using them very successfully in the early stages of mayfly hatches. No matter what insects the soft hackle patterns are supposed to imitate, they work. Obviously, soft hackles, because of their universal appeal also represent very good searching patterns when there are no hatches.

I suggest putting a few of these spiders in your fly box.

Hunting Tigers

Angel and I have been hunting tigers unsuccessfully for several years. We began our hunt for tigers in the in the shadow of Bald Mountain at Willard Pond. I am not talking about feline tigers but the piscine tigers better known as Tiger Trout.

The tiger trout is a sterile, intergeneric hybrid of the female brown trout and the male brook trout. The name derives from the pronounced vermiculations, evoking the stripes of a tiger. Tiger trout have been reported to grow faster, be more aggressive, and fight harder than other trout.

Our hunting ground on this trip was Lucas Pond in Northwood, New Hampshire. It is a 53-acre pond with an average depth of 25-feet, the deepest hole being 58-feet. The shoreline is fairly well-developed.

Angel and I drove to Northwood and found Lucas Pond Rd., usually a good sign for finding a pond. The topo map was not very clear as to exactly where the access was located. We reached the end of Lucas Pond Rd. and turned right in the direction of the pond, then turned on a dirt road leading us to private camps on the shoreline. Two fishermen told us the public access was, in fact, back on Lucas Pond Rd. They were going to go to the landing to escape the bugs that were eating them alive, and to follow them. Sometime just finding a new pond is an adventure.

We launched our float tubes into the wind and waves. The two fishermen that directed us to the landing told us they were catching fish in a cove up the right hand shore. Angel said he would head for that cove. I decided to fish a cove to the immediate right of the landing. It looked promising because it had a brook draining the pond.

It was hard to tell depth because the water was tea-colored. I managed to hook several largemouth bass in the cove. It is not easy landing bass on a barbless trout flies, one jump and the bass would go one way and the fly the other.

When I got to Angel's cove we decided to move to a smaller and more sheltered pond. We caught no trout and the wind was really whipping. As we got to the landing, Angel saw a fish swirl on the surface. We fished for a short while. Angel kicked to shore and took out. I made my final cast and began to reel in my Black Madonna fly.

Looking over my shoulder, selecting a spot to take out, my fly stopped with a jolt. Line began emptying from the reel as a fish headed for deeper water. We could not see the fish in the stained water. Several minutes later I was able to work the fish to the surface. It was very silvery, clearly not a bass. Rainbow, I called out, no Angel corrected, no red stripe. Salmon? I questioned, no again, as Angel pointed out that there were no salmon in the pond. As I slipped the net under the fish I could clearly see the worm like markings of a brook trout on the fish's back. My first Tiger Trout.

Snook After Dark

The side-arm cast propelled the fantail chartreuse Clouser far up under the dock. It landed with a loud splat in the blackness of the night. A spotlight on the dock was focused on the water and lit a circular area ten feet in diameter. I drew the Clouser into the light. Close behind was the haunting silhouette of a large fish following the fly. In my mind I could hear the melody from "Jaws." The fish easily overtook the fly—the fly disappeared—I set the hook—the fish exploded and ran for deeper water.

Bill and I were snook fishing with our host Bob, of Cape Coral, Florida. Bob lived on one of the canals and told us that people placed spotlights on their docks to attract snook. These snook lights attracted bait fish which then brought in the predators.

One night after cocktails and a pleasant dinner, Bob suggested we check out a few of the nearby snook lights. Bill and I grabbed our fly rods before Bob could change his mind. We walked out to Bob's dock and loaded our gear on board his boat.

Bill was first to fish. Bob navigated the boat to a cast away from a circle of light. Bill cast his fly to the center of the light circle. Bob said it was best to cast beyond the light into the darkness and retrieve the fly into the light. This advice came a little too late as a snook dashed into circle and almost ripped the fly rod out of Bill's hand.

We fished several more docks containing these snook lights with mixed results. Most circles of lights housed a snook or two.

Others showed no signs of the predators. Bob said these barren circles of light might have been new lights that had not yet attracted a resident population of baitfish or snook.

Not everyone wanted to share his or her spotlight bounty. Several docks had motion detectors that would cause lights to come on and illuminate their entire dock and yard. This may have been more for security reasons rather than to discourage fishermen. One of the homes clearly wanted to keep fishermen away. As we stealthily approached this snook light, the motion detector set off not only the security light but also a water sprinkler set up at the end of the dock. We quickly backed away laughing at the shower we received.

As we approached the next light, it was my turn to fish—but this is where we came in.

Warren Hatchery

"Looks like a stocking truck," I said jokingly, as we caught a glimpse of a white truck around the bend of the road. Angel and I were on a gravel road leading to Long Pond in Benton. We originally went to Oliverian Pond but the wind was whipping the surface into white caps. I recommended we try Long Pond because it is a long narrow pond running north and south and would be protected from the west wind.

As we got closer to the truck, we could read "WARREN HATCHERY" across the back. We looked at each other and grinned. This was going to be a good day. The hatchery truck parked near the pond. We started to suit-up and get our gear assembled. As we were preparing to launch out float tubes, a Conservation Officer drove up towing a boat. This was going to be an in-season boat stocking.

We got talking with the conservation officer, Greg Jellison, about local fishing conditions. As we were about to launch, we were asked politely to show our fishing license; Greg remarked that he had never found any fly fishermen without one but he still had to check.

As we fished away from the landing, the warden launched his boat and the hatchery truck backed down to the water. Two large buckets were filled with water from the truck and brook trout were loaded into the buckets. We watched as the boat and its contents sped around the bend to the far end of the pond. This was repeated several times over the next hour or so. On his last trip, he dumped a bucketful of fish between Angel and me. The hatchery truck drove off and Greg loaded the boat and departed. It was just Angel, me, and the brookies.

The fish were boiling on the surface. This was going to be like shooting fish in a barrel, or so we thought. We cast to nearby risers. We cast to nearby risers time and time again, no response. It wasn't very long before the trout stopped rising. Long Pond is very shallow, average depth of 4-feet with an 8-foot deep hole far to our south. Those brookies simply disappeared. Angel said this happened to him a couple of times before; the freshly stocked fish take a couple of days before they start feeding again.

Again we spread out and cast blindly for holdover fish. By the end of the day, we were able to catch a couple of brookies apiece. It was a pleasant but slow day of fishing. At least we were able to fish on this very windy day.

On the drive home, we waved as we passed the WARREN HATCHERY.

Tim Pond

Several years ago, my friends, Bill and Jack, invited me on a fishing trip. Jack's family and friends have a long-standing tradition of going to Tim Pond Camps every year on Father's Day weekend. Tim Pond is nestled in the breathtaking beauty of the western mountains of Maine. The camp is the oldest sporting camp in New England, having hosted guests since the mid-1800s.

Immediately upon arrival, we were served a lunch consisting of soup and a huge sandwich. Dining is a special treat at Tim Pond, providing three home-cooked meals daily. After lunch we partnered up, grabbed our gear, and jumped into one of the classic Rangeley Boats that are available for guests, and began fishing the mile long pond. The pond has never been stocked, and offers a plentiful supply of colorful native brook trout.

Bill, my afternoon partner, had been here before and he took me to his favorite spot. We fished streamers under the surface and had some pretty steady action. I heard a bell ringing. Bill told me it was the supper bell as all the boats began rushing back to dock. I don't remember exactly what supper was, but I do remember it was enormous and was followed by a large strawberry shortcake.

My evening partner was Neil, Jack's father-in-law. We motored out to his favorite spot. As we dropped anchor, mayflies began coming off the surface. Shortly a caddis hatch joined the mayflies. At dusk it looked like it was snowing, with the flakes rising instead of falling. The fish were everywhere; the water was boiling with rising trout. Neil told me to save a fish for breakfast.

The next morning, after fishing with Jack, I was served my trout along with eggs Benedict. The following two days were pretty much repeats of the first day.

Bill and I returned in September for the final week of fishing. In the fall, the camp shifts from fishermen to hunters. The owners, Betty and Harvey Calden, have been operating the camps since the early 1980's. Betty said that the hunters eat three times as much food as the fishermen. The hunters would eat a ½ dozen eggs and fixings for breakfast, then pack 4 or 5 sandwiches' for lunch, and return hungry.

I returned, with my fishing companions, several times over the years and have always had fun, good fishing, great food and wonderful company. Rocking chairs on the porch of each cabin are available for enjoying the peace and quiet, but being a fisherman, I saw no need to rock away a big meal.

Are We There Yet?

The black Lab ran ahead of his master to check out the strange looking figures, two men carrying float tubes on their backs. "How much further," I asked the dog's master, with a heavy breath and a stitch in my side. "You're almost there—only a couple hundred more feet," the stranger assured. The black Lab decided we were harmless and continued down the path.

"Are we there yet," lingers in your mind when you have been on the trail longer that the amount of time you mentally calculated to cover the expected distance. A steady uphill can raise havoc with any calculation.

I was still musing about the number of cars at the trailhead. I expected to have the hike-in pond to ourselves, especially mid-week. There were three cars parked at the trailhead, and a fourth car pulled up as we began to unload our gear. It was a father and son, also fishing the pond for the first time.

Angel and I had been planning to fish Cole Pond for three years. It held special interest for us because it is a hike-in, fly-fishing-only pond. Willem Lange on NH Public Television featured it on Wildlife Journal. In fact, Angel had been communicating with Willem about the pond.

Shortly after passing the black Lab and his master, we came to the pond. It was a beautiful pond in a beautiful forested setting, well worth the effort of getting there. In fact, two of the cars were just enjoying the area.

The pond is located in Enfield Wildlife Management Area, in Enfield, New Hampshire. The pond itself covers 17-acres. It's deep pond with a 54-foot deep hole and an average depth of 25-feet. Seeing the pond and being eager to get fishing, we recovered quickly. The float tubes were pre-inflated allowing us to be on the water in short order.

I saw a riser to my left, so I kicked in that direction. I cast to the area of the rise and had several light taps on my fly. It wasn't long before I had a fish on, but turned it into a LDR (long distance release). The father and son launched their belly-boats. In a few minutes the father yelled, "Fish On." After landing the fish, he announced it was a sunfish.

Angel and I circled the pond, catching small sunfish—very disappointing. We each managed to catch one brook trout apiece; Angel got a 4-inch brookie, still with its parr marking indicating an immature fish, and I caught an 11" brookie. At least we didn't get shut out.

Time for our descent, much easier going out but the mosquitoes seemed thicker. At the end of the trail, a partridge ran in front of me followed by five fist-sized yellow chicks. She went into her injured act, crying and dragging her wing. We left the partridge family to their business.

We packed the car and started the long ride home. I wasn't long before Angel asked, "Are we there yet?"

North Country Bass

A fish swirled behind the pulsating yellow-marabou tail of the oversize Zoo Cougar. I re-cast my fly to the exact spot where the fish had swirled. The water opened and the fly disappeared in a large whirlpool. I set the hook but the fish had hooked himself with the vicious strike. A large largemouth bass rose straight out of the water and shook its head attempting to throw the hook. The bass towed me around for several minutes before I could get control.

I was fishing Burns Pond, in Whitefield, for the first time. Angel and I were on a tour of North Country bass ponds. We fished the shallow cove for a couple more hours without any more interest from any additional bass. We decided to move on to a nearby pond.

We drove over to Forest Lake. As we looked at the large lake, the wind picked-up. The water was clear and looked like it was a deep lake—not very promising. I noticed several navigational buoys that I thought might indicate shallow areas. Angel and I looked at each other and decided we might as well give it a try because we were there and it was a body of water we had never fished before.

I launched my float tube and kicked away from shore. Immediately large rocks appeared on the bottom of the lake. "Looks like good smallmouth water," I said to Angel. I had a few light hits on my orange Zonker before I finally managed to hook a small sunfish on the large bass hook. A few casts later the fly met the strong resistance of a foot long smallmouth bass. Things began to looking-up.

I worked the rocks with the orange, rabbit-strip, Zonker. As I retrieved the fly in short strips, alternating with short pauses the fly stopped short and a large smallmouth rocketed out of the water. The smally turned out to be another large fish. A very good day indeed.

A couple of plastic-bottle floats caught my eye, I moved toward them. As I approached the markers, the bottom dropped away. I changed my fly to fast-sinking chartreuse Clouser. The fly had large weighted eyes and would sink fast. I cast between the two floats. A bass will often hit a lure as it is sinking through the water column. The fly line started to move to my right; I set the hook to something very heavy. For a moment I thought I was hooked to the bottom. Shortly the line began moving to the right. Several minutes later, I worked the fish close enough to see it was a largemouth bass, a real surprise in this smallmouth water.

I lifted the fish out of the water and could see the fish was solidly hooked in the bony part in its mouth. The lip showed signs of previously being caught. I gripped the fly with my forceps and badly bent the hook releasing the large bass. I placed the fish back in the water and watched it slowly swim away. Great day fishing for North Country Bass.

Knife to a Gunfight

I heard about Martin Meadow Pond a couple of years ago while fishing Mirror Lake in Whitefield, New Hampshire. When the fishing slowed, other fishermen would say they were going to try Martin Meadow Pond, just up the road.

The Topo Map indicated the pond to be in Lancaster, off Rt. 3 on Martin Meadow Pond Road opposite Weeks State Park. *The Field Guide to Trout Ponds of New Hampshire* by Paul VanderWende listed fish species as Rainbow Trout, Smallmouth Bass, Largemouth Bass, Pickerel and Horned Pout. Any pond with both warm-water and cold-water game fish sparks my interest. The guidebook listed its characteristics; Acres 118, Max Depth 30', Mean Depth 13', and Clarity 10'.

I was on my annual fishing trip to the Great North Woods of New Hampshire. Every year in October my buddy and I, head up to Colebrook, rent a room at the Northern Comfort Motel and eat at Howard's Restaurant. This is our idea of roughing it; warm room, hot showers and eating like kings. We would fish the local ponds and streams, and then on the way home try a new pond. This year it would be Martin Meadow Pond.

It was cloudy with a light rain falling as we turned into the gravel launch area. The half-dozen-car size parking lot was empty; we had it all to ourselves. The shoreline looked to be minimally developed. As we inflated our float tubes, I saw a washtub size swirl just to the left of the landing and dimples far out in the deeper water. Promising.

The landing cove was very shallow with lily pads along the shore. I cast to where I saw the large swirl and got a light hit immediately. On my second cast I hooked a small pickerel. The main goal was to catch some rainbow trout, so I kicked for deeper water where I had seen the dimples. At the head of the cove I caught a small smallmouth bass. In the deeper water a fish hit my white Zonker. A rainbow trout, I hoped, but my deep-felt suspicions were confirmed. The dimples were yellow perch.

The sky darkened; the rain increased, and thunder could be heard in the distance. It was time to head back. I fished the edge of the weed-bed on my return.

The weed-bed held pickerel. I managed to land a couple of small pickerel on my light trout rod with 4X tippet (.007" dia.). But it was no match for adult pickerel with a mouth-full of razor-sharp rows of teeth. I watched the larger pickerel, with their razor-sharp teeth, bite the fly right off on the first strike. It could hear them telling me, "Don't bring a knife to a gunfight."

Stonehouse Pond

Angel and I drove up and down Rt. 201 in Barrington, looking for Stonehouse Pond Road. On the third drive-by, hoping it was not someone's private entrance, I turned onto an unmarked dirt road that appeared to be in the direction of Stonehouse Pond. Later, we found out someone had removed the road sign. The road led us to a parking lot with a capacity for a dozen cars. Three cars occupied spaces. I jumped out and climbed up above a small hill and gazed at the pond. "Angel, wait till you see this—this is probably the prettiest pond we ever fished," I called back.

We took in the beauty of the pond for a few moments. We looked out from a small cove across the 14-acre pond to a far shore overpowered by a huge granite cliff. Two canoes were on the pond, working the far shore.

According to *"The Atlas of New Hampshire Trout Ponds"*, Stonehouse Pond is 14-acres in size, with a 30-foot average depth and 48-feet in the deepest spot.

Angel and I were quickly on the water; eager to see around the two points of land that defined the sheltered cove we were in. There was not much more of the pond than we could see from the launch area. To the west, was a shallow cove with aquatic plant and a marsh like shoreline. To the east, was a lovely forested shoreline.

At the mouth of our launch cove, I caught my first brookie. It was a brilliantly colored fish with its dark olive body, orange belly, and white, black and orange fins.

I fished toward the western cove and picked up another fish on same soft hackle spider. One of the canoes had moved into the west cove, I directed my float tube toward the granite cliff. This area appeared to be very deep, the cliff continued directly into the water. There were several fish working the overhanging bushes.

A group of youngsters arrived. Several of them walked a path along the eastern side to the cliff and others sunned themselves on the rocks by the landing. A couple of women launched kayaks and toured the pond. Obviously this was more than just a great looking fishing spot; it was also a great recreation spot.

As we pulled out of the pond around 5 o'clock, several cars pulled into the parking lot; all fly fishermen. It appeared that the pond was a favorite with the after-work crowd.

Don't know why it's called Stonehouse Pond, might as well be called, Beauty Pond, or Pleasure Pond, or better yet, We'll-Return Pond.

Knives for Fun and Profit

I was first introduced to the utility of a knife in the Boy Scouts. My Ulster multi-bladed, black-handled official Boy Scout knife enabled me to always BE PREPARED. The black-handled knife allowed me to quickly cut a rope, carve a fuzz stick or slice a finger. I carried the knife everywhere, including middle-school, if you can believe that. In High School the black-handled official Boy Scout knife was replaced by a Kay-Bar pocketknife that I continued to carry to school, a different world.

Over the years, I added many knives to my collection; so as to be prepared: a Swiss Army knife, a marlinspike knife for my sailboat, and several fishing knives. I have knives made by: Bone, Buck, Case, Cattaugus, Diamond Edge, E Blyde, Gerber, Ka-Bar, Opinel, R J Richier, Ulster and Victorinox.

My long-time favorite is a small Case fixed-blade fishing knife that I carried on my belt for many years. I also prize my father's Ulster folding-fish-knife with a slim blade, fish-scalar and hook-dislodger. My most collectible knife is a handmade knife made by one of the pioneer custom knife makers, Ralph Bone, from Lubbock, Texas.

One day after fishing the Androscoggin River, my fishing buddy, Bill and I stopped in a fly-fishing shop in North Conway. Bill asked about gravel guards for his waders and was told he was in luck because Ted, an Orvis representative, was in the store. Ted introduced himself. During the conversation with Bill, Ted eyed the sheath knife on my belt. He asked if he could see the knife, he was a collector. I handed him my forty-plus-year old Case knife.

Ted examined the knife and asked if I wanted to sell it. My immediate reaction was not to part with the knife for sentimental reasons. Again, he asked how much I would want for the knife. Not knowing the value of the knife, I again said I was not interested in selling. Ted then said he had a nice little Orvis, 1 weight rod, reel and line in his truck that he was willing to swap for the knife. Bill estimated the value of this offer to be between seven and eight hundred dollars. Not needing another rod and not knowing the true value of the knife, I declined the offer. I wanted to keep my old friend, the Case knife. Ted handed me his card and said if I change my mind to give him a call.

I haven't looked up the price of that knife, or care to even know it. That rawhide-handled knife is now safely stored with all the other knives in my collection.

The Squawking Gull

A sliver of light appeared on the eastern horizon. As morning broke and the light grew skyward, we could see the beach was lined with fishermen. Mike, my brother-in-law, and his three sons, Ray, Jason, John, and I were standing on the beach at Race Point, Provincetown, Massachusetts. We had driven out in Mike's well-equipped Chevy Blazer the previous evening and fished for strippers during the night. We got a few hours of sleep in the sand-buggy and were now trying to work out the kinks and get the blood flowing.

All of a sudden, we could see birds gathering about a 1,000 yards south of us. We could see the fishermen running toward the beach. A shoal of bluefish was chasing baitfish along the shore heading toward us. We removed our rods from the rod rack and ran to the shoreline. Birds were diving and the bluefish were beating the surface into foam. The boiling patch of water approached us as the shoal of bluefish continued to tear into school of baitfish. We watched as the line of fishermen hooked fish as they passed and moved northward toward us.

Mike was about 100 feet south of me and was first of our party to get a blue on the line. I cast straight out from the shore into the melee. I watched as my lure shot into the sky and started to fall leaving behind an arch of line. As the lure was about to land in the water, a herring gull flew straight into my line. The line looped around the gull's wing and it flew straight up towing my lure behind it. The bird had little purchase in the air, and was easily reeled in. The gull was screaming, the bluefish were boiling, all the fishermen were fast to fish, and I was fouled up with a herring gull.

The bird landed on the beach about 10 feet away from me. I carefully approached the bird and assessed the situation. But the age of miracles hadn't passed; with my nephews restraining the struggling, nipping gull, I managed to cut the lure free and un-tangle the line from the bird's wings. The unhappy gull was safely released. Without any thanks, and a loud squawk, the bird flapped its wings and flew off to join the feeding frenzy.

The blitz of blues was passing by. With trembling fingers, I fumbled my gear together. I made a side arm cast, keeping my line low and out of the way of feeding birds. As soon as the lure hit the water a bluefish hit it. I fought the fish for a few minutes. The blue shook the hook out, but another bluefish immediately hit it. I was glad that I didn't completely miss the action struggling with the squawking gull.

Skin Your Eyes

I watched a school of brookies as they cruised across the 2-foot deep sandy flats. I stealthily approached the target. I cast my fly six feet in front of the school of brookies and as soon as the fly landed, one of the lead fish shot forward and nailed the fly. This was repeated over and over for several hours. I was fishing one of the ponds in the Great North Woods, when I found these fish cruising the shallows.

One of the best features about fly-fishing is that it can be a very visual sport. It is always exciting seeing a fish rise to a dry fly, but being able to see a fish in the water, before you cast to it, is the height of visual excitement.

There are some conditions that provide opportunities of sight fishing. Spring may find fish swimming along the surface or shallow coves searching for mayflies or caddis flies. Summer can find them cruising for dragon and damselflies. In the fall, they can be seen along the shores or inlets preparing to spawn.

One should always be on the lookout for signs of action on flat water. Sometimes a fish can even be seen on the surface with their heads, dorsal fins or tails out of the water. This condition allows easy sightings. The most difficult conditions are when the trout are fully under the surface. It is these conditions that require the most attentiveness. When the trout are just under the surface they may have a slight effect on the water's surface. This condition is known as, "nervous waters," and may resemble a cat's-paw caused by a slight breeze.

I have had some wonderful days casting directly to sighted fish. The best opportunity for successful sight fishing is obviously in clear waters. Here in New Hampshire we are blessed with many lakes and rivers with low turbidity levels.

There are certain techniques that can be best applied to spot fish. Obviously the higher you are the easier it is to see in the water. This is not always possible in a boat or canoe. The flats boats in Florida are equipped with raised platforms for poling and spotting fish. This height problem is severe when wading or in a float tube where one is virtually in the water.

The sun's position is critical for the best position for spotting fish. Try to position yourself for the best visibility into the water. Polaroid glasses are a must. Amber lenses seem to be best at highlighting the fish.

Watch for movement or shadows cast against the bottom. The ability to spot fish can be improved with practice. Of prime importance is attentiveness. As Captain Ahab said about Moby Dick—"skin your eyes for him; look sharp."

T8R9

The Cessna 185 circled the pond once, and then dropped down to buzz the moose out of the pond. On the third pass, Matt Libby gently touched the water and with only one bounce glided the plane to shore. Bill and I jumped out and unloaded our gear. Matt pushed off and motored to the center of the pond, revved the engines, and flew away. Bill and I were all alone, miles from civilization.

We watched the plane disappear over the horizon. Feeling a little deserted, Bill said, "Oh well, let's get started." We launched the camp-canoe that was stashed on the shore and pushed off. The pond was shallow with ample aquatic growth. It was a very hot day, 95°, with a blazing sun high in the sky, conditions not favorable for brook trout.

There were a few rising trout and we were able to catch a few fish. Bill managed to get one nice wild brookie in the 17-inch range. In desperation we paddled into nursery cove, noted for its abundance of small fish. Well it must have been "Nap-Time," because we did not catch one of the little tykes.

Back at camp, Matt, our host, said, "This is definitely a forgotten spot in Maine," sweeping his arm gently across the panorama of Millinocket Lake. "People think, oh, Millinocket Lake, I've been there," Libby said, "But they're referring to the lake south of Baxter Park and don't realize there are two Millinocket Lakes."

Libby Camp is located in T8R9 in Maine's Great North Woods. Northwestern Maine is divided into Minor Civil Division's, MCD's. These MCD's divide Maine's unincorporated area into numbered Townships and Ranges. The nearest town, Ashland, is forty-five minutes away by unforgiving logging roads.

The next day, Matt flew us to a deeper pond that held, not only brookies, but, land-locked salmon as well. The weather remained hot and sunny. We fished nymphs on sinking lines and were able to catch a few fish. As we waited for the flies to sink, we watched a pair of loons hop on and off their nest, tending their chicks.

Each day, Matt would fly us into a pond, and, at the end of the day, fly us back to the Main Camp. There are eight guest cabins and a lodge at Libby Camps. The guest cabins are handcrafted of peeled spruce and balsam fir, and furnished with homemade or antique beds neatly covered with homemade quilts, woodstoves, propane lights, flush toilets and showers. Meals are served family style, and the talk is all about fishing, exactly what we wanted.

Leather Tail

On a warm and sunny spring day, while driving north on Rt. 132 in Sanbornton, I noticed several ponds along the road. Whenever I drive by water, I wonder what kind of fish live there. The ponds alongside the road all appeared to be warm water ponds and promised to hold largemouth bass and pickerel. I made a mental note of these ponds for future reference.

In the dog-days of summer when the trout are all down by the thermocline and hard to reach with a fly line, my fishing attention turns toward bass and pickerel. I heard about bass fishing in Hermit Lake from two separate sources. I looked up Hermit Lake in the New Hampshire Atlas & Gazetteer and was surprised to see it lying beside Rt. 132 in Sanbornton.

The Gazetteer indicated, starting from the south, Rollins Pond, Cawley Pond, Hermit Lake and finally Pinnacle Pond in Meredith along this route. The sign for the Pinnacle Pond public landing is actually labeled Spectacle Pond, causing a bit of confusion.

I had a couple of new bass flies I wanted to try out. The first was an improved Zonker. It consisted of a white rabbit strip wing and a red hackled head giving the fly a larger profile. The white and red, colors of the Polish flag, has yet to be named. Maybe the "Falcon?" The second fly was described in the summer issue of the *Fly Tyer* magazine and was called the Leather Tail. It is a large 4 to 6-inch fly and designed to be easily cast on a light rod. The fly has a long narrow strip of leather with a palmered (wrapped) rabbit-hair-strip body to give it some bulk. Since I use my light 5-weight rod for bass I am always developing large flies that cast well.

The Sanbornton Town beach was empty as I launched my float tube. I stripped out some fly line and began working the line out. The "Falcon" landed about 30 feet out over the clear sandy bottom. As I stripped additional line off my reel, a large bass swam out of the nearby water lily patch and inhaled my new and improved white and red fly.

Later I changed to the Leather Tail to check out its casting and fish-catching ability. I was very pleased with its castability and action in the water. The long leather tail squirmed and twisted as the fly was retrieved. It had plenty of life-like motion in the water, irresistible to even a well-fed bass. After a few short hits, I trimmed an inch or so off the 6" long tail to prevent fish from just grabbing the tail. This improvement allowed me to catch a yellow perch along with additional largemouth bass and pickerel. There will definitely be more Leather Tails in my fly box on the next bass outing.

Whenever I drive by water, I still wonder what kind of fish live there and look forward to someday returning and fishing these mystical bodies of water.

No Trespassing

"NO TRESPASSING"—"NO TRESPASSING"—"NO TRESPASSING"—
the signs repeated every 100 feet or so. Like Burma Shave signs
stacked up alongside the road, but all with the same message.
Finally my father, Uncle Henry and I, came to an open area under
a power line, with no posting. We were acting on a tip, searching
for access to an "Ice Fishing Hot Spot," in central Massachusetts.
The pond was reported to be producing a lot of big pickerel and
perch.

We pulled the car off the road and unloaded our fishing gear.
The traps and gear were loaded into a box mounted on runners,
allowing us to pull it over the snow and ice. About twenty minutes
later we reached the shore of Mud Pond. We selected a spot and
started to set up our traps.

We got a couple of traps set up, baited with minnows, when
we saw a Massachusetts State Police cruiser pull up beside the
pond. The state trooper got out, and started walking toward us.
He was dressed in his leather boots, jodhpur style pants, and stiff
brimmed drill-instructor hat. "Oh—Oh here he comes," my
father said. Now, we were expecting something like this, as we
had been warned that the owner of the posted property wanted
to keep this pond to himself, even though he did not own the
entire shoreline.

The state trooper, all spit-shined and warmed from his heated
cruiser, approached us. He pulled out his citation book and

started to write us up for trespassing. "Wait a minute," my uncle said, "we came in over un-posted land." The officer said he was told the entire shore was posted and had already issued several citations. Walter and Henry offered to show the trooper our route and prove it was un-posted. Off they went, re-tracing our route through the three feet of snow that lay on the ground.

I was left behind to continue setting up our tackle. Before I could set up all the traps, flags started to go up. I ran from trap to trap hauling in some large pickerel. Flags were popping up as fast as I could catch a fish, re-bait the hook with a shiner, and re-set the trap. About an hour later, after I had almost caught our limit of five pickerel each, I saw the three adults returning. The trooper was wet and cold. The snow had filled his leather boots and had fallen behind his shirt collar and soaked his shirt. He had not been properly dressed for the trek through the snow-covered, power-line route, and had paid the price. The state trooper apologized for attempting to cite us for trespassing, and said, "I'm going back and tell that guy never to call me again."

Snapper Blues

The red and white bucktail hit the water with a loud splat. The fly hung in the current for a moment. A twitch of the rod tip caused the bucktail to dart left then right. A silver missile shot up from the depths and swallowed the imitation baitfish. The rod bent, the fish jumped. Another snapper bluefish for supper.

Pat and I, along with another couple were returning from an afternoon at Horseneck Beach, in Westport, Massachusetts. We had spent a pleasant September day walking along the sandy beach and enjoying a picnic lunch, washed down with cool Bloody Marys. Malcolm, our host/guide, who grew up in the area, suggested we stop and fish the Westport River for snapper blues. He said they should be in the river at this time of the year and would make a tasty evening meal.

The bluefish is a popular game fish found along New England's Atlantic coast. The bluefish has a moderately stout body and prominent canine teeth. The "snapper," or young bluefish is slightly deeper and more flattened in appearance than the adult. The snappers exhibit the same aggressive behavior as the adult. They are voracious predators that will attack fish half its own size.

We drove north on Rt. 88 and turned onto Old County Road. We parked in a turnoff area near the bridge that crosses the Westport River. The tide was going out causing a fast current in the river. Malcolm said the conditions should be good for fishing.

We rigged our fly rods and walked down to the river's edge. The two women watched us from the bridge. It wasn't long before the red and white bucktail worked its magic. The second baby bluefish took the silver tinsel off the fly; the third snapper took off the bucktail. I tied on a yellow and red, Mickey Finn, and got the same results.

The sharp teeth of the aggressive snapper blues destroyed several more streamers. Soon we had half a pail full of fish. Malcolm and I cleaned the fish, and got them on ice for the ride home. Bluefish are an oily fish and should be cleaned immediately, iced down, and like sweet corn eaten that day. The snapper's flavor is milder than the adult bluefish.

That evening, we concluded a very pleasant day at the beach with a feast of fresh-caught snapper bluefish and more Bloody Marys.

Trigger Flies

I side-arm cast a large gaudy-yellow Zoo Cougar under an overhanging tree branch; the fly landed with a loud plop. The three inch long fly pulsated for a second. I began stripping it in. The fly shot forward three times, a slight pause, another series of quick forward movements, followed by another pause. On this last stop, with the marabou tail waving just below the surface, a lunker brook trout shot up like a submarine launched cruise missile and inhaled the fly.

Kelly Galloup wrote about this phenomenon in his book *Modern Streamers for Trophy Trout*. He explains trophy fish feed on large prey mostly in low-light (night) conditions and spend their days under cover. Kelly goes on to write, that a large bait-like fly behaving like an injured or frightened food source will invoke a reaction, hard to resist an easy opportunity for a quick meal. Think, a cat resisting a string. He referred to this type of flies as, Trigger Flies.

This method was intended for catching large fish. I once had a monster largemouth bass hit a pickerel that was struggling on the end of my line. My fishing log indicates that small and medium size fish will react to Trigger flies. I have seen foot-long brook trout chasing and attacking struggling salmon smolt.

Galloup's book contains patterns of these Trigger Flies, including the Kiwi Muddler, Butt Monkey, Woolly Sculpin, Stacked Blonde, Madonna and my favorite, the Zoo Cougar.

Zoo Cougar recipe:
Hook: Streamer style hook
Thread: Danville, yellow
Tail: Yellow marabou
Body: Pearl Sparkle Braid
Underwing: White calf tail
Wing: Yellow mallard flank feather
[tied horizontally]
Collar: Yellow deer body hair
Head: Yellow deer body hair,
[clipped muddler style]

These trigger flies can be tied in various colors to suit different situations. My fly box holds several of these trigger flies. I carry a yellow Zoo Cougar, a tan neutral-buoyancy Madonna and a black cone-head Madonna. I doubt I need to spell it out; Trigger flies will improve your chances of catching that trophy trout.

Open Water

Every winter end, I get the urge to go fishing. I see the white-winter ground start to turn brown, the snow gently receding revealing ribbons of gun-blue water flowing through the gray frozen surfaces of streams and lakes. Time to start scratching that fishing itch.

I pulled my float tube from its winter stowage position in the rafters of my garage. Next I stripped the floating line off the reel and discarded it. At the end of last season it cracked about 30 feet from the tip; the most critical area. I loaded a new, heron-colored, very-high-tech, fly-line on the reel. I sewed a Pemigewasset Trout Unlimited patch on my vest. I was ready to go.

On a beautiful warm sunny day, I put on my long underwear and fleece pants anticipating water temperatures in the thirties, and loaded my stuff in the car. I pointed the car toward Mirror Lake in Woodstock. This is a non-managed trout pond and can be fished prior to the 4th Saturday of April, opening day of managed trout ponds. I like to test all my gear before the opening of Trout Ponds; this field trip allowed time to fix or replace any non-functioning gear.

I turned into the public landing only to be greeted by a field of snow. The lake was completely ice bound. Now what? I pulled the New Hampshire fishing regulation booklet out of the glove box and searched for a non-managed trout pond further south. Winona Lake. I pointed the car south.

On the first sighting of Winona Lake, the lake appeared to be socked in with ice. But a couple of acres of the south end of the lake were ice-free. I checked the outlet stream and saw a half-dozen very-large suckers in their spring colors beginning the spawning session.

I suited up and launched my float tube. As I kicked away from shore, a flight of swallows passed overhead, a promise of warmer days to come. I fished the shallow cove for a couple of hours; careful to avoid piloting my float tube close to the sharp edges of the ice, remembering what happened to the Titanic.

Not even one hit. But catching a fish was not really the main purpose of this trip. My float tube held air, my waders successfully kept the icy water on the outside and I scratched that fishing itch.

White Pond

"Straight across 16?" I asked. "Straight on 171 to 28 north, then south on 16 for a quarter of an inch," Angel read off the topo map. We were on our way to fish White Pond in Ossippe. I pulled off the road to get a mental picture of where it was I was going. "White is off 171!" I said, "You gave me directions to Duncan Pond." "Oh well—I didn't have my glasses on." Angel responded.

Angel was telling me about how the Wampanoag Indians of Massachusetts were about to get approval to open a casino. "I think we passed the road to White," I said, "too busy talking." I turned the car around and turned down an unmarked gravel road.

The parking was limited at the public access. I parked so as not to block the boat trailer access to the sandy landing. We opened the doors and were immediately seized by a swarm of mosquitoes. Angel immediately put on some kind of mosquito-condiment to give his blood a deet flavor, while I passed on the sauce for all those mosquitoes that prefer their blood au-natural. The mosquitoes continued to eat us as we put on our waders and assemble our rods. We were on the water in record time, pushed by the biting insects. Fortunately, the mosquitoes did not follow us on the water.

White Pond is one of the few ponds limited to fly-fishing. I was a little surprised to find houses and camps on half the shoreline. Most fly-fishing ponds are located in undeveloped, secluded areas. The pond is 47-acres with an average depth of 23-feet with the deepest hole being 36-feet. The pond holds both eastern brook trout and rainbow trout. A local resident told us it used to be a good hornpout fishery, but the pout disappeared.

I kicked left to fish the east side and Angel kicked right. We agreed to rendezvous at a specific time and compare notes. I had a few light hits after only a few casts, but they proved to be small perch. As I kicked along the shore, I could see a school of small perch following my fly. Through the clear water I could see a sterile bottom, no rocks or weeds, devoid of structure.

Catching only perch along the shore I decided to try deeper water, if only to get away from the perch. From a distance, I watched Angel hook a fish; when he reached for his landing net I knew it was a game fish. He later told me it was a rainbow trout. He said he must have dropped the fly on the rainbow's head, because the fish hit as soon as the fly hit the water.

Later when we met at the appointed time, we decided to leave White Pond. Although we were told by other fly fishers it was a good pond, it was not good to us that day. Besides it was time to feed the mosquitoes again.

May—A Gentle Month

May is a gentle month. The hillside's light-green colors of exploding buds have turned into the dark-green color of mature leaves. The spring gunmetal-gray color of water has turned into the summer deep-blue. The dead-leaf brown of the forest floor has turned into the various colors of wildflowers.

May is a gentle month for fish. The waters have warmed to preferred temperatures for the fish. Insect life is active. There is plenty of food for hungry trout trying to make up for the cold months behind them.

May is a gentle month for fishermen as well. Mild, long, spring-like days of bright sunshine prevail. Cold feet and stiff fingers have been all but forgotten.

May is the month that gave Mayflies their name—they have a gentle look about them. Anglers dream about these hatches.

One day on Tim Pond, in Maine, my companions and I fished the daylight hours with a modicum of success. The supper bell rang and every boat raced for the camp. After a feast of stuffed pork-chops, mashed potatoes and mixed vegetables followed by a wide slice of freshly baked blueberry pie, we headed out for the sunset fishing session.

We anchored off an inlet in about four feet of water. Soon the first mayflies rose from the surface. A few trout began to rise. At dusk it looked like it was snowing in reverse. The water was boiling with rising brook trout.

On another occasion, while fishing Pennsylvania's Fishing Creek, I witnessed more species of mayflies hatching at the same time than ever before. March Browns, Cahills, Hendricksons, Sulphers and Green Drakes all exploding off the water simultaneously. Trout were in a frenzy. Anglers were frustrated because their fly on the water is one of thousands. Getting to have a trout select your fly was like hitting the lottery. Breaking down our gear in the dark, we found the car completely covered with mayflies.

One day while fishing the Newfound River, on a warm May afternoon, Mayflies danced above the river below an overhanging tree, the Light Cahill spinners dropped to the river surface to deposit their eggs, trout eagerly waiting below. This is one of the many pictures I have in my mind, of the gentle month of May.

The Last Cast

I prefer lakes that hold both largemouth and smallmouth bass; it increases the chances of catching fish. Largemouth and smallmouth bass belong to the same family but are quite different in appearance and behavior. The closed mouth of the largemouth extends beyond the eye while on the smallmouth the closed mouth extends to the eye The largemouth is green in color, with a distinctive wide-black stripe along the lateral line; the smallmouth is brown in color, hence its nickname "Bronzeback." The largemouth can be found in and around aquatic plants; the smallmouth live around rocks. The largemouth can tolerate warm water; the smallmouth prefers cooler water.

On my last trip to a bass lake, I started with a floating line and large neutral-density fly, working the shore for bigmouth bass. I dropped my fly close to shore, let it rest a moment, and then retrieved it in short strips. I worked my way up the shore, picking up a couple of small to medium sized largemouth bass.

As I entered a shallow cove, I saw a pickerel follow my fly. I changed to a large chartreuse Zonker style fly adding a short wire shock-tippet to handle the barracuda-like teeth of the pickerel. I managed to land, with the help of my net, several pickerel.

When I reached the end of the cove and deeper water, I switched to a sink-tip line and a weighted bucktail fly. I planned to work over some rocks submerged in eight to ten feet of water. This looked like great smallmouth territory. The ledge extended a long way out from shore and was marked with navigation buoys. I fished along the drop-off, alternating casting onto the shallower and deeper water. This method paid off with a couple of nice smallmouths.

At the end of the day, I found myself back at the boat landing. I had had a good day; always happy to catch a Grand Slam (one of each type of game fish). I made my last cast and started to reel in my line. Suddenly the fly stopped short, my rod tip dipped into the water and a largemouth exploded out of the water, best fish of the day. There seems to be something magical about that last cast.

On the Water

The telephone rang, "Are you on the water?" Angel asked. It is his opening line whever he calls. "No," my usual answer, but I knew he was ready to hit the waters again.

We decided to fish a pond in the Pine River State Forest, Effingham, New Hampshire. A dam on Wilkinson Brook, a tributary of Pine River, forms the long narrow pond. The pond is very shallow with an average depth of 4-feet and an 8-foot deep hole. It appeared to me like a glorified beaver pond especially with its heavy tea-stained water.

My third cast to the dam produced a hit. I pulled in the 6-inch fish with ease. "Angel . . . guess what this is? . . . You'll never guess." "Salmon?" he called back. "Pickerel!" I replied. My third cast resulted in another small pickerel. Angel called over, "you always seem to catch the unexpected fish," as he set the hook. He fought it to the surface, "brown trout . . . no . . . it's another pickerel," Angel reported.

When a third pickerel was caught, I decided to change flies. I figured if the pond had pickerel it most likely had largemouth bass as well. I removed the small nymph imitation that had caught the two small pickerel and replaced it with a larger, tan-colored Madonna streamer. This fly would be better for larger pickerel and bass and would catch brook trout if there were any around.

I found myself on a shallow shoal, about a foot deep. My flippers were touching the bottom as I kicked for deeper water. I cast to the grassy flat and got an immediate hit. This was a heavy fish—n ot like the hammer-handle's I had been catching. As I got the fish close, I still could not tell what was on the end of my line. The fish towed me around protecting its identity in the stained water. As the fish tired, it came to the surface and I saw it was a large brookie. The fish was almost black from living in the stained water and muck bottom. The fish was very wide; obviously well fed (. . . maybe eating small pickerel.)

Several casts later, I had a sharp, quick hit. When I pulled in my line to check my fly, I discovered the fly was missing. A pickerel bit the fly off with one bite. We were fishing for trout. I did not have a wire leader on my leader as I would if I were fishing for pickerel.

Angel and I continued catching pickerel after pickerel all afternoon. Some of the pickerel were of respectable size. We lost count of the flies that were completely destroyed or bitten off by the pickerel. It was a good chance to clean out our fly box of old-little-used flies. Interspersed among these freshwater barracuda were more of the wide-body, dark brookies making this a great day on the water.

Return to Freedom

Freedom, New Hampshire, is a small village located along the Maine border. Freedom is home to, a fly-fishing only pond. The pond has a slot limit; fish between 12 and 16-inches must be immediately released. A limit of 2 fish, with only one fish over 16-inches, can be kept. Fly fishermen keep very few fish from fly-fishing only ponds, and the ponds tend to hold fish all year long. Shawtown Pond is where I caught my first trophy size brook trout.

I decided to finish the trout season on Shawtown Pond. I kicked my float tube north, toward the shallow weedy cove where I saw a riser. After a half-hour without a hit, I caught something that dove into the weeds and got off. As I brought my weed encrusted fly toward me, I saw two lunker brook trout following the weed ball.

I continued to work the area. Occasionally a huge brookie would swim under my float tube. They had no interest in anything I threw at them. Finally I got a fish to take my fly; a beautifully colored 17-inch brook trout. I fished my way slowly toward the shallower water and noticed clear patches of gravel full of circling trout.

Now I understood; the squaretails were on their spawning beds and had no interest in eating. I could see a half-dozen fish circling nearby. I knew I had to try something completely different because none of the flies I had fished had attracted any attention from the fish.

I tied on a heavily dressed Zoo Cougar, thinking maybe a floating fly would trigger a reaction. I cast the floater about five feet to the right of the pod of lunkers, gave the fly a twitch and three of them raced to the fly. The winner got to the barbless hook first and got his picture taken before being released.

Thinking I had finally figured out the secret to success, I continued casting the Zoo Cougar and the fish continued to ignore the fly. The fish hitting the fly on the first cast was a fluke. I decided to leave the brookies alone on their gravel redds and go home after a very pictorial day of fishing for some oversized brookies. In my mind, I made a note in my log-book to return earlier next year before the trout got on their redds and were still interested in food. I shall return to Freedom.

Cold Close

It was a cold close to the end of New Hampshire's trout season. Snow had covered the ground along with the red, orange and yellow trees just two days prior. The morning of October 15th, the last day for fishing, was prematurely cold with temperatures in the twenties. The snow remained in the higher elevations of the mountains surrounding Waterville Valley.

I dressed as warmly as I possibly could and still have enough flexibility to cast a fly. Fleece socks and pants, long underwear, turtleneck, heavy shirt, topped off with jacket and rain coat and waders to keep dry.

The float tube was inflated to the max, allowing for the shrinkage the cold air and water would have on the inflated air. I strapped on my fins, on the dry land to avoid getting the hands wet in the chilly water. I backed into pond and gently sat down in the float tube. The water temperature registered forty degrees, five degrees below the minimum temperature that trout remain active.

I stripped line off the reel and cast the fly. I worked the pond's margin with my fly, casting cast after cast searching for a hungry trout. The wind bit my face and hands; the cold crept through the waders, fleece socks, pants and long underwear. The cold penetrated all my armor.

A tug on the line, a splash on the surface, a tight line, a bent rod and a leaping rainbow trout was an instant furnace. All of a sudden my hands and feet glowed with warmth.

In a way, the cold close of the trout season was a nice way to end the year. The cold made it easy for me to stow away my fly fishing gear for another six months.

Nets

Bill slid the oversized brook trout across the surface, to over the long-handled boat net that I had strategically placed in the water near the canoe. I lifted the net. The net rose a couple of feet above the surface of the water, but trout continued thrashing in the water. Bill and I looked at each other in complete puzzlement. The old cotton netting had rotted and could not support the weight of the fish: the large brook trout had broken through the net. We managed to land and release the brook trout but we learned a lesson that day, cotton netting rots with age.

Nets, I have had a few. Over the course of my fishing career, I have owned, used and worn-out several landing nets. I first used a tiny net to retrieve shiners from a bait-bucket. Then came the larger boat nets. Nets with long handles and wide hoop openings to easily scoop any fish we managed to catch and safely transfer them to a stringer for later consumption.

It was when I started fly-fishing that my net collection grew. I acquired a smaller, more portable net for use while fishing ponds and rivers. This net was simply a miniaturized version of the boat net. The nets had snaps that attached to a D-ring on the back of my fishing vest and was always ready for quick deployment.

This deep-netted trout net was replaced with a "catch-and-release net." This net differed in that it had a small mesh and shallow pocket: the shallow pocket was designed so that the trout would not be severely folded, potentially causing harm. The netting was a much finer mesh, again to be more fish-friendly. The latest trend is to have rubber netting, so as to not remove any of the protective coatings of the fish.

I remember my uncle, Stanisław making nets from the same type of cotton twine that rotted out in Bill's net. He taught me the craft of making nets. Stanisław left me his home-made wooden shuttles and gages because I was the only one interested in the dying art. I still have the old, home-made, wooden shuttles and gages.

Skunked

I cast the lure out, counted to four, and set the hook. That's how easy it was. My father and I were into the largest school of large white perch we had ever seen. We easily filled a pail with huge white perch.

Earlier in the day, Greg, the owner of the Grand Lake Stream Fishing Camp where we were staying, asked us if we would catch him a mess of fish for a fish-fry he planned for his visiting family the next day. He shared his local knowledge and told us where we could easily catch a mess of fish. Dad and I quickly agreed.

The next day, as we drove into camp, we could smell the fish cooking and hear the merriment of the family gathering. Greg rushed over to greet us and invited us to the fish fry. He introduced us to his extended family and offered my father a drink. It was obvious, even at my young age, that all the loud merriment involved a lot of beer and whisky.

After more food and drink, Greg started to tell us some of his stories. He told about fishing and hunting in Maine and about some trapping experiences. He went on to tell about a skunk that had visited his trap. Greg said that the animal's leg was bruised but otherwise was fine. He then invited us to see the animal.

We followed Greg to the barn. He shined a light into a crate. We could see the skunk huddled in the back. He put the light down, opened the cage, reached in and removed the animal and began petting it.

He asked me if I wanted to hold it, and before I could respond he carefully placed it in my arms. With slurred words, he said, "If his leg h-heals—I w-will give him a name and get him fixed." GET HIM FIXED! I looked around to determine the direction to throw the skunk and run, but I remained steady. Greg knew how to handle the animal; he had wrapped the tail under the skunk when he handed it to me. Greg gently took the animal from my arm and placed it back in the crate. I quickly exited the barn and left the skunk in the dark.

More than once I have been skunked fishing, but this was the first time I came close to really being skunked.

Fishing Guides

When I was a youngster and learning to fish, my father was my guide. Fishing hot-spots were found by searching for them. Hours were spent checking out fishing holes and actually being on the waters fishing. Sometime, with luck, tips came from an underground network of fishing buddies.

In my many years of fishing, I have only had a few professional fishing guides. The first was in Labrador. Labrador law requires fishermen to hire guides to prevent visitors from killing themselves by getting lost in the wilderness or eaten by bears. It also provided jobs for the local residents.

Marcel, my Labrador guide, ferried my fishing partner, Charlie, and I to various fishing locations on the lakes and rivers. Marcel spoke French and a little broken English and was happy to leave the fishing decisions to us; he was there primarily to keep us safe.

The local chapter of Trout Unlimited recommended my second guide, Rocco Rosamilia, of Keystone Anglers, Lock Haven, Pennsylvania. He specialized in guiding fly fishermen on chalk streams. Fishing with Rocco was not like having a guide; it was more like fishing with a long-lost friend. I returned to fish with Rocco and cast those classic Catskill dry flies to rising brown trout.

I had a couple of guides in Florida. The first one put my companions and me over a lot of fish, including a six-foot Tarpon.

The second guide—not so much. I knew we were in trouble when he showed up with bait on a fly fishing expedition.

Now-a-days there are fishing guide services everywhere. There is an Orvis endorsed guide service a few miles down the road from my house. Occasionally I see Richard Bernard, of Fin Fighters Guide Service, fishing Profile Lake with his very-happy clients.

I have been asked to do some guiding but I enjoy fishing too much to put down my rod and watch someone else fish. I once guided a recuperating friend who was too weak to fish by himself. I brought him to a small pool in the river that I knew held fish. Catching a rainbow and two brookies brought a smile to his face. I knew my buddy could have found these trout on his own when he was stronger but for a short time it felt good to be a fishing guide.

Urban Trout

Living and working in the Quincy area, just south of Boston, provided limited fishing opportunities. The Old Swamp River was 10 minutes from my house. It was far from a picturesque place, not likely to be seen on any calendar. I have often said that trout only live in beautiful places, but the Old Swamp River was an exception. It was one of few places I could easily fish after working a long day, a place I could grab some semblance of the natural world and clear my mind of the day's labor.

The headwater of the Old Swamp River is in Rockland, Massachusetts. The river runs through South Weymouth, under the south-bound lane of Rt. 3, westerly for a short distance between the divided highway, northerly for a couple of hundred yards and flows into Whitmans Pond. From there it flows through East Weymouth where it becomes the tidal Back River emptying into Quincy Bay and Boston Harbor.

The access from the main road is through a gravel pit. On the back side of the gravel pit, a path leads to the section of river between the divided highway of Rt. 3 and Whitmans Pond. The path ends at what I called the "Truck Tire Pool." The small gravel bottom pool held two partly submerged truck tires. Above the pool was a short riffle area and above the riffles was what I called the "Bed-Spring Pool." Yes—someone had discarded their bedspring in the river. Above that pool was the culvert under the north-bound lane of Rt. 3.

The times I fished the river, I would walk up to the Rt. 3 culvert and fish downstream. If I could avoid snagging the bedspring, I had a good chance of catching a rainbow. For some reason the Truck Tire Pool was a favorite place for brown trout. Below the Truck Tire Pool, the river slowed, widened and deepened as it entered the pond. This section held several types of game-fish; a trout on one cast, a pickerel on another, maybe a largemouth bass, all hungry for a meal.

Although the Old Swamp River was not picturesque, when I fished I had the river to myself and was luring some large, lovely urban trout.

Ritz Crackers

As I fished along in my float tube one fine spring day, I turned to see where I was going and noticed a long thin object on the surface of the water. On approaching the object, I discovered a white fly line. I reached out and got hold of the line and started pulling it in. On the end was a rather large gaudy fly. I continued pulling the other end until a fly rod and reel appeared. The custom made rod was recently built for the owner. Curiously the automatic fly reel dated back to the 60's.

I circled around and could see more fishing gear lying on the bottom, in about 10 feet of water, much too deep to reach. As I was leaving and packing my gear, my friend Charlie, drove into the parking area. I told him about the rod and scattered fishing gear. Charlie told me that a canoe had tipped over and the two fishermen lost their gear. I posted a note about retrieving the rod, along with my telephone number.

I returned a week later to do some fishing and was surprised to see the gear still on the bottom. Obviously no attempt was made to retrieve the gear. I had no response from the notice I posted.

I could see a pack, white bucket and a couple of mushroom anchors in the 10 foot depths. I attempted to snag the pack with my fly, but was unsuccessful.

The next time I returned to the pond, I was prepared with a large-hooked jig in case the pack was still there; it was. With the large-hooked jig, I was able to snag the pack. It turned out to be a large fanny-pack containing a box of flies and two additional automatic fly reels that matched the reel on the rod. A sleeve of well-soaked Ritz Crackers was also in the pack. Clearly someone's treasures.

Mid-summer and my notice of the found rod remained at the boat landing. The bucket and mushroom anchors remained on the bottom. Clearly no attempt had been made to retrieve the gear.

Maybe the owners were from out of state. Maybe the trauma of overturning a canoe was too much for them, and they gave up fishing. I still have the gear, minus the Ritz Crackers.

Return for the Tigers

Willard Pond, located in the dePierrefeu—Willard Pond Wildlife Sanctuary in Antrim, is high on my list of favorite ponds. High because the pond's water clarity is among the best of New England lakes, and a shoreline that gives the impression of a wilderness pond and its tiger trout.

Huge boulders deposited by receding glaciers, an unusual mixture of trees and plants, and an abundance of wildlife make this sanctuary a unique and attractive area. The pond holds brook, rainbow and tiger trout, as well as a population of smallmouth bass. Chances of one species being active are pretty good.

On my last trip, the tiger trout were actively feeding. As I launched my kick-boat, I watched a concentration of fish feeding in a shallow cove. I navigated to the edge of the cove and cast my fly to the center of the cove. Bingo! The first Willard Pond tiger trout.

As I was bringing in my second fish, I felt a presence behind me. I turned and saw a pair of hungry-looking loons about 15 feet off my starboard side. I quickly muscled in the fish and released it. One of the loons swam under my float tube and the other loon dove and swam in front of me. In the clear water, I watched the loon's black and white backs circle me looking for an easy hand out.

With mixed emotions, I resented the loons harassing my fish, after all I was there first, but on the other hand, how many times do you get this close to loons. I held my fly out of the water as the pair of loons swam under and around me for several minutes.

When they finally departed, there were no rising trout to be seen. A little disappointed I started to move to deeper water. Within a few minutes after the loons departed, the trout began rising again. I moved back into the cove and continued to cast to the feeding tigers.

During the day, as I fished along the shoreline, the pair of loons came to visit me several times. They would swim around and under my float tube, and I watched them chasing fish. You have to see the speed that loons can achieve, to believe it.

I think it is this type of experience and the overall beauty of the Audubon sanctuary that keeps Willard Pond high on my list of favorite ponds, and keeps me returning for the Tigers.

My Biggest Bass

The biggest bass that hit my lure was one that I never actually caught. Let me tell you about my biggest bass encounter. One hot-sunny summer day, I was fishing a shallow-weed-infested cove in search of pickerel. I was in my float tube in about two to three feet of water, casting huge flies into the aquatic vegetation along the shore.

I cast my fly to a small opening in the rushes. As soon as the fly hit the water there was a boil about ten feet away followed by a wake heading directly toward my fly. I set the hook and the fish dove into a bed of native milfoil. I thought I would lose the fish but it was well hooked. I managed to pull the fish free of the weed bed.

I could see it was a medium-size pickerel, covered in a ball of milfoil. As the pickerel struggled, I noticed the rushes moving. Something was deliberately moving toward my pickerel weed ball. Looking closer I saw the head of a largemouth bass pushing the rushes aside.

The bass swam into the clearing and continued straight toward the struggling pickerel. I could clearly see it was a huge bass. The bass slowly moved in and grabbed my weed-covered pickerel sideways in its huge mouth and began slowly swimming off with the fish firmly in its mouth.

The bass must have felt the resistance of my line because it suddenly released the pickerel. I watched as the bass slowly swam into the cover of the weeds. The bass must have been between eight and ten pounds.

I landed the pickerel, removed the plant material and examined the fish for any damage. The ball of milfoil protected the fish from the bite of the bass. I unhooked the pickerel and released it, so it could tell its story of its double escape.

I tied on the biggest-baddest fly I had and fished the foot-deep water where the bass swam after releasing its noontime meal. I kept hoping it would return and hit my fly. My fly must have looked pretty puny compared to the 15-inch fish the bass had just released. That largemouth bass was definitely the biggest bass I never actually caught.

Black Water

In the low-angle light of October, the pond surface appeared to be made of polished obsidian—the black water perfectly reflecting the mirror images of the yellow, orange and red of the autumn leaves. A breeze changes the polished surface. The obsidian surface acquires silver-colored jimmies of reflected light. Increasing breezes slowly reverses the surface from black to silver.

The beauty of the fall season comes at a cost, cold winds and cold temperatures. Ear warmers and turtlenecks are the dress code of the day. Rain gear is worn, even on sunny days. I don't want a splashing trout to get my sleeves wet. Fleece pants are worn under the breathable waders. Gloves come out of storage and no sock is too heavy to prevent the cold from creeping in.

Brook trout have left the cool depths of summer for the shallow shoals. They are searching for food and preparing their redds. Rainbow and brown trout move in closer to shore to ambush the minnows, dace and crawfish. Predator fish are preparing for life under the ice.

The dry fly box along with the floatant bottle and drying pad are set aside. No need for flies that mimic mayflies and caddis flies as that season is long gone. A few midges and flying-ant patterns are retained for any serendipitous fall hatches. The streamer box comes into its own; full of minnow, dace and crawfish imitations.

October 15th is the culmination of the trout pond fishing in New Hampshire; the last hurrah so to speak. The weeks of October witness the transition from the kaleidoscope of colors to the browns and grays of pre-winter. Falling leaves float on the pond surface and collect on the lee shore.

I finish out the season by completing a circuit of my favorite ponds, one last visit to places that provided so much joy during the year, one last trip to the black water.

Billingsgate Shoal

John, my brother-in-law, pointed to the low pile of rocks and long sand bar and said "That's all there is left of Billingsgate Lighthouse and Island." Billingsgate Island Lighthouse was built to mark Billingsgate Island and the entrance to Wellfleet Harbor, Massachusetts. The Light was decommissioned and the island became completely submerged by 1942. Today, Billingsgate Shoal is a sandbar that appears only at low tide and is marked by a Lighted Buoy Fl G 2.5s, Lighted Buoy Fl R 2.5s, Lighted Horn Buoy Fl G 4s, Lighted Bell Buoy Fl G 4s, and a Red nun Buoy.

John, Laura (my 16 year old red-headed niece) and I were on a lookout for signs of fish. We looked for diving sea birds, jumping bait fish or just plain nervous water. Occasionally the fish finder indicated a fish at the 23-foot depth. The plan was to locate some stripers or bluefish and bring them in close to the boat with large plugs and then switch to the fly rod.

John and Laura cast their lures at several prime locations while I stood by with my fly rod at the ready for any sign of fish. Nothing. We moved to deeper water and fished the drop-off at the south end of the shoals.

Again nothing. We decided to do something completely different. We dropped the anchor. John and Laura dug some nice fresh cherrystones for appetizers. Back on the boat, I saw some round objects moving towards us. As they got closer, I could see that the objects were seals. Over recent years, the seal population has increased ten-fold in Cape Cod Bay. At the north end of the shoal, we saw dozens of seals frolicking in the water or just sunning themselves on the rocks and sandy beach.

A few more casts at the mouth of Wellfleet harbor produced nothing. Catching a bluefish on a fly was not in the cards that day. No complaints. After all, how many chances do we get to have a boat ride on a beautiful summer day in Cape Cod Bay?

We watched a fog bank roll in until visibility was reduced to yards. We followed the GPS's bread-crumb track back to the harbor. Laura played the part of a Boatswain's Mate, putting out the fenders and attending lines in preparation to re-attaching the boat to the truck. Back home, the cherrystones were opened, cocktail sauce mixed, and a family feast began. Pizza, not fish, was our supper that day.

Squam Lake

Squam Lake, aka On Golden Pond (site for the movie), is a pristine lake located in Lakes Region of New Hampshire. Originally, Squam was known as Keeseenunknipee, which meant "the goose lake in the highlands." In the early 1800's, the lake was given another Abenaki name, Asquam, which means water. Finally, in the early 1900's, Asquam was shortened to its present version, Squam.

Squam Lake contains many species of fish; salmon, rainbow trout, lake trout, largemouth bass, smallmouth bass, pickerel, white perch, yellow perch, hornpout, whitefish, cusk and smelt. The lake covers 10.5 sq. miles with a 60-mile long shoreline. Its deepest spot is 98-feet deep, with an average depth of 36-feet. This is one place were average depth is misleading as there are rocky shoals far from shore.

One can fish for cold water species, salmon, rainbow trout and lake trout in the morning and for largemouth bass, smallmouth bass, pickerel and other warm water varieties in the afternoon.

Bill and I spent many sunny days fishing for Squam's smallmouth bass. We would cast oversized streamers tight up-against shore and strip-retrieve them. Often the fly would land with a splat and a bass would attack the fly with a washtub size whirlpool. Very exiting. Most of the 60-mile shoreline is strewn with rocks that hold bass. There are many submerged rocky reefs in the middle of the lake that can hold smallies in the heat of summer.

On warmer days, we would move out to the shoals and cast full sinking lines to these submerged rocky reefs. Smallmouth love rocks. Find a bunch of rocks and you will find smallmouth.

Moving into some of the shallow coves is like moving to a different pond. These coves contain aquatic plants and fallen trees along the shore and are perfect habitat for largemouth bass and pickerel. The largemouth bass hang out by docks or other large woody debris that dot the shore of these shallow coves. Pickerel can be found in and around the patches of lily pads.

Bill and I fished and explored most of Squam Lake and were always on the lookout for Jane Fonda, Purgatory Cove, and "Walter," the humongous trout.

Special K

I was sitting at the computer thinking about what to write for my one-hundredth *Fins & Feather* article when the phone rang. "Ray, this is Pete . . . what was that orange fly you gave me a month ago?" Pete went on to tell me that he just came off the river, and after a hitless hour and a half, decided to try something completely different. He looked in his streamer box and saw the strange orange fly I had given him. On his first cast he caught a brookie, on his second cast a 20" rainbow inhaled the orange fly and broke-off with his only orange fly. He told me he was heartbroken. "What was that fly?" Pete pleaded.

That orange fly was something I created almost a half century ago. If memory serves me correctly, the fly was inspired by a classic bass fly called the Brown Bomber. The fly caught my eye because it had very little brown; it was mostly orange. Classic bass flies have large silhouettes and it was that silhouette that attracted me. The proportions of my creation were significantly different from traditional trout bucktail streamer flies but slimmer than classic bass flies. I tied the fly with a tongue-in-cheek attitude and flippantly called my fly The Orange Mother and later The Orange Muddler.

To my surprise the fly caught trout. It not only caught trout, it caught a lot of trout. The fly caught land-locked salmon, brook, rainbow, brown trout, as well as largemouth and smallmouth bass and every type of pan-fish. It did exceptionally well in ponds that held crawfish. The fly became my "Go-To-Fly," when nothing else seemed to work. It was time to re-think the name for something more permanent and serious.

The fly I gave Pete was my own, "Special K." Over the years I have given the fly to many fishermen who had similar experiences. If you tie flies, tie up a couple but be warned don't go out with only one.

Special K recipe:
Hook: Streamer style hook
Thread: Orange
Tag: Brass wire
Tail: Orange calf tail
[As long as hook shank]
Body: Orange floss
Rib: Brass wire
Throat: Orange calf tail
[To end of hook, 30° stand off]
Wing: Brown calf tail
[To end of hook, 30° stand off]
Collar: Yellow hackle

Catalogs

Thoughts of spring fishing begin to creep into my mind just as the fishing catalogs creep into my mail box. I can't resist looking at them as they arrive. The catalogs describing rods vastly improved from the year before that were vastly improved from the year before that. After all these years of improvement the rods should be able to cast a fly by itself or at least notify you that your fly is heading to a tree on your back cast.

Catalogs that describe fly rods made from "patent-pending thermoplastic, thermoset resins used from tip to butt with a woven-graphite and gold-anodized aluminum skeletal reel seat" costing well over seven hundred dollars. Rods designed to be faster, lighter, longer and with more pieces every year. All attributes going opposite of my preferences. I prefer two-piece, slow action rods of less than nine feet.

Reels "machined from aircraft-grade aluminum bar stock," with drags that are smoother than a baby's bottom, costing hundreds of dollars. Reels anodized in bright colors, some resembling the color of the trout they were designed to catch. Manufacturers ignore the fact that trout reels are used primarily to hold the line when not actually casting.

Catalogs loaded with lines designed for all occasions, for cold temperatures, for hot weather and more tapers than one could conceive. Lines with textures; Sharkskin, Dimples and Grooves.

Lines specifically designed for one specific species of fish. Enough choices to make your head spin.

Waders, rubber bottom wading boots, vests, gadgets and tools fill the pages of these catalogs. Not to mention all the high-tech clothing designed especially for outdoorsmen. Despite the fact that I don't need, or even want, any new gear I enjoy pouring through these catalogs to see what's new in the field. I especially like to see what new flies are for sale, even though I only use the same half dozen flies over and over.

March catalogs fall into my mail box like snowflakes; covers depicting fly fishermen wearing bulging vests, logo hats all in exotic places, holding huge fish. The catalogs awake a feeling for open water, where I can cast a fly and watch for a rising trout.

The Cruelest Month

T. S. Eliot once wrote "April is the cruelest month". April in New Hampshire is a neither season; neither winter nor spring. Days where mid-day corn-like snow freezes into gray boilerplate ice at night and with the last remnants of deep snow slowly changing to mud; it is a shoulder season.

April may be a cruel month but it marks the beginning of open water fishing. River and streams are beginning to lose their ice covering. Swift, Roaring and Mad Rivers reveal the origin of their names during the snow melt. Air is still cold; water colder still. Wading feet and legs are cold and numb. Ice in the guides must be melted with stiff fingers every few minutes. Water is high and turbid and trout remain lethargic in the cold water.

The call "ICE OUT!" goes out to all the fishermen who fish the big lakes for land-locked salmon. Salmon are a true coldwater fish preferring 30° to 40° temperatures. The salmon have moved into the shallows chasing smelt and are vulnerable to top-water anglers.

Ice is usually off the smaller ponds by Opening Day, but not always. One year, I drove to Franconia Notch to find a half-foot of snow in the parking lot. Another year, I arrived at my favorite pond only to find a multitude of fishermen looking out over a pond that was still ice-covered. Yet another year, I piloted my float tube away from the sharp-edges of ice flows, trying to avoid another Titanic situation.

April may indeed be a cruel month, but it is time for us anglers to cast those flies we have tied during the winter onto the water in anticipation of fooling our adversary. It is time to again clear our minds of everyday things and concentrate on presenting a fly in an appropriate manner. A few cold digits are a small price to pay in order to cast a fly in the cruelest month.

Holiday Hex

It happened at lunch during the 4th of July weekend. Pat and I brought some long time friends, Norman, his wife Bobby, their daughter Mellissa and granddaughter Emily to our favorite eatery (the Squam Lake Inn) for lunch. Our friends live in Marietta, Georgia, and this was Emily's first trip to New Hampshire. We toured some of the White Mountain National Forest's famous attraction; The Flume and Old Man of the Mountain Memorial.

While we enjoyed our delicious lunch, it happened. I looked out the window and saw a sight that makes a fly fishermen heart race and fills him with anticipation. There sitting on the building was an extremely large yellowish-cream mayfly. The legendary Hexagenia Limbata.

As soon as our guests departed for Georgia, I was on my way to my favorite pond in search of New Hampshire's, and the world's, largest mayfly. I arrived around six o'clock thinking I would fish a Hex nymph imitation under the surface with my sink-tip line and a bead-head fly. Two hours later, with the sun below the trees, I had a couple of hits and one LDR (Long Distance Release). There was still no sign of a hatch. Around eight o'clock I decided to switch to my floating line and tie on a yellow and cream colored, size 6, dry fly the size of a small hummingbird.

As darkness fell, the Hex nymphs began to rise to the surface showing small dimples on the surface. The dimples broke and the high visible yellow sail-like wings appeared. Hexagenia mayflies rose gently in the air to propagate their species on their one day on earth.

Soon whirlpools appeared under the hatching Hexagenia and loud slurps could be heard as the trout began to feed. As darkness set in, the night sky was filled with silhouettes of the rising mayfly duns. Loud splashes were heard around the pond. Trout smashing their prey immediately to my port and starboard and under my rod tip. In the darkness fly-fishing changed from visual to audio as I reacted to the sound of any splash in the vicinity of my fly.

The Holiday Hex hatch was on!

White Oak Pond

I am constantly on the look-out for new waters to fish. A friend was telling me that he fished at a local pond and was having fun with the bass. I inquired as to which pond it was?

He said, "The pond at the end of Shepard Hill Road." I was familiar with the road but not the pond. I checked my topo-map and sure enough there was White Oak Pond. It even indicated a boat launch area.

The pond was not listed in any of my fishing reference book or the Fishing and Game web-site. I am not sure why the pond did not register in my mind when I searched my maps as I often do.

The next time I was in the area, I drove to the end of Shepard Hill Road and sure enough there was a pond. It looked promising. The sign at the launching site indicated that it had parking limited to 4 cars, and a 7½ hp limit on boats. A chain was across the ramp, restricting it to key-holders. It became clear; the launch site was intended for canoes and kayaks.

Whenever I go to new water, I usually go with a friend. None of my fishing buddies were available and because I checked out the pond and knew exactly where it was, I decided to go alone.

My reconnaissance indicated a warmwater fishery, so I came prepared for bass and pickerel. I rigged my 5-weight trout-rod with a heavier leader and tied on a bass-size fly. The launch cove was narrow and long. When I cleared the cove I could see some homes, some very large homes, on the north shore. I decided to fish the less-developed west shore.

I was casting into the lily-pads trying to attract a bass or pickerel that may be lurking waiting for lunch to swim by. I happen to look down, and in about 4-feet of water, I saw the largest snapping-turtle of my life. The enormous turtle was just lying motionless on the bottom. I gave several strong, swift kicks to get away from any potential danger to my float tube.

The pond was about 250 acres, a little large for my float tube. I managed to cover about ¼ of the west shore, catching a couple of decent-size pickerel. I worked my way back fishing the deeper water off shore, with little success.

Later that day, my log entry recorded the time, date, place, wind speed, water temperature and the two pickerel caught on a white Zonker. It also recorded a loon sighting and the worlds-record snapping turtle.

Invitation

I awoke with the intention of going fishing, but an October temperature reading of 34.9° cooled that idea. As I sat by the fire catching up on my reading, the phone rang. It was Allen, inviting me to go fishing. I told him I thought it was a little too cold and dismissed that idea. He said, "Don't worry it will warm up by noon." I reluctantly agreed to accept his invitation as there would not be many more fishing opportunities this year.

I arrived at the pond around 11:30 am, to find Al constructing a new leader. I helped him with the leader and gave him some 4X tippet. We finished rigging up and launched my float tube and Al's kayak. The sun was shining and the pond was calm; the mirror-like surface reflecting the white clouds, blue sky and orange hillsides.

We fished along the shoreline for an hour or so before I caught a nice brookie. We were at the far end of the pond, when the wind kicked in. Al and I decided to move to the lee shore. This shoreline held some large boulders. "Good smallmouth bass water," I said confidently.

Shortly I felt a sudden jolt at the end of my line and set the hook to something heavy. A big smallmouth flashed through my mind. Shortly the fish surfaced and showed the dorsal fin and back of a very long trout. The golden flash of color told me it could be a brown trout. The fish jumped a couple of feet out of the water confirming the identification.

Al was close by to witness the epic struggle between man and beast. I untangled my net and slid it under the brown trout. I hoisted the trout up to the apron on my float tube. The apron has an 18-inch ruler imprinted on it and this fish overhung the ruler by a couple of inches on both sides. This was the largest fish of the season.

Al pulled out his cell-phone and took a couple of quick pictures prior to me slipping the golden-colored monster back into his realm. I was glad I didn't stay in my warm and cozy realm. Life is short, accept invitations.

Fishing Log

Several years ago my nephew, Ray, gave me a leather bound log book with "Uncle Ray's Fishing Memories," engraved on the cover's brass plaque. It is the most elegant fishing log I ever owned—something Ernest Hemmingway would be proud of.

Memories play tricks with times and dates. Seasons get jumbled. Locations are confused. Facts replaced with wishes. Fish grow larger. My entries record data in real time.

I record the usual information a fisherman would want to recall: date, water fished, water temperature, air temperature, wind speed, wind direction, weather conditions and any and all fishing companions. The quantity and species of fish caught, and the names of the flies that caught them.

I also note all wildlife of interest. Eagles swooping out of nearby trees, osprey diving for fish, loons, kingfishers, great blue herons, huge snapping turtles, otters playing, black bears trying to sneak away and moose standing in the river below me are all entries.

Also included in each entry is anything of particular interest that happened. e.g. "saw the snake swimming across the river. Trying to clear my fly out of the way, accidently snagged it in the back. Got the snake to shore, and with two hearts beating fast, and as gently as I could, removed the barbless hook. We each went our separate ways."

I recommend all fly fishermen to keep a log as memories of time and places blur with time. Allen, one of my fishing companions, shared his log book eloquent entry of our last fishing trip of the year together:

No hits or fish for me,
but Ray caught three.
Two Browns and a Brookie,
the . . . Brown was Ray's
biggest of the year.
The Special K did its trick,
so all I had to do
was take the pic.
What better way to spend
a day than with a friend.